HOW TO MANAGE YOUR CAREER

In this Series

Other titles in preparation

MANAGE YOUR
CAREER

Achieving your goals in a changing workplace

Roger Jones

How To Books

By the same author in this Series

How to Emigrate
How to Get a Job Abroad
How to Get a Job in America
How to Master Languages
How to Retire Abroad
How to Teach Abroad

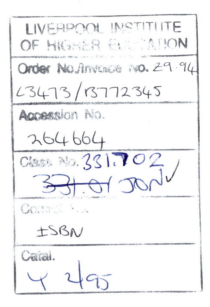
British Library Cataloguing in Publication Data
A catalogue record for this book is available from the British Library.

© Copyright 1994 by Roger Alan Jones.

Roger Alan Jones has asserted his moral right under the Copyright, Designs and Patents Act, 1988 to be identified as the author of this work.

First published in 1994 by How To Books Ltd, Plymbridge House, Estover Road, Plymouth PL6 7PZ, United Kingdom. Tel: Plymouth (01752) 735251/ 695745. Fax: (01752) 695699. Telex: 45635.

All rights reserved. No part of this work may be reproduced or stored in an information retrieval system (other than short extracts for the purposes of review) without the express permission of the Publisher given in writing.

Note: The material contained in this book is set out in good faith for general guidance and no liability can be accepted for loss or expense incurred as a result of relying in particular circumstances on statements made in the book. The law and regulations are complex and liable to change, and readers should check the current position with the relevant authorities before making personal arrangements.

Typeset by Concept Communications (Design & Print) Ltd, Crayford, Kent. Printed and bound by the Cromwell Press Ltd, Broughton Gifford, Melksham, Wiltshire.

Contents

List of Illustrations

Preface

The past fifteen years or so have been a time of extraordinarily rapid change. The aspirations of people everywhere have been turned upside down and old notions subjected to reappraisal. Individuals are having to come to terms with the disconcerting prospect that they can no longer expect to progress smoothly upwards in their career.

This is a time of uncertainty where employers seem to come and go with increasing rapidity; jobs disappear without trace to be succeeded by new trades and professions which did not exist a decade ago. No wonder there is a mood of bewilderment among employees and those who are about to enter the jobs market.

There are, of course, some excellent handbooks on specific careers designed with young people in mind, and other books offering advice on job interviews and job applications, but they are limited in scope. A person's career is essentially a lifelong process in which landing a job forms only a part. There are other matters to be considered as well, such as how to be successful at your workplace and knowing when or whether to move on.

In a time of change it is no longer possible just to hope that something will turn up. Rather than relying on chance you need to take charge of your destiny. Indeed, you will need to engage many of the disciplines that a good manager deploys, such as decision making, measuring risks, and planning. I have therefore called this book *How to Manage Your Career*.

People who manage their careers effectively are much less likely to get blown off course by the ill winds of recession and the onset of change. For this reason this book should have something to offer people of all abilities and all ages. Whether you are sixteen or sixty you too can achieve a satisfying and successful career — but only if you *manage* it.

Please note that the words 'company' and 'organisation' in this book are interchangeable and denote any corporate body which employs people both in the private and public sectors. The words 'job' and 'position' are also used in their broadest sense and are not indicative of status, although in other contexts they may be, as the following quotation shows:

> The humblest of applicants seek 'jobs' or 'vacancies', while the more ambitious are looking for 'places', 'posts, 'positions' or 'opportunities', note Derek Torrington and Laura Hall wryly. 'The really high fliers seem to need somewhere to sit down, as they are offered 'seats on the board', 'professional chairs' or 'places on the front bench.'[1]

Whether you aspire to a job, a position or a seat on the board of a major company may I wish you every success with your own chosen career.

Roger Jones

[1] *Personnel Management: A New Approach*, Derek Torrington and Laura Hall (Prentice Hall International UK, 1991).

1
Why Careers Need
to be Managed

What on earth is happening? In the early 1980s a shock wave went through most Western economies. Massive redundancies occurred in industries that had been regarded as the bedrock of the British economy for decades, such as ship building, mining and car manufacture. The unemployment rate shot above the three million mark, with Scotland, Wales and the North of England particularly badly hit.

Then — for a while — things started to look better. House prices rose by leaps and bounds, young people just out of college landed themselves lucrative jobs in the financial service industry, and the yuppie lifestyle was born. Companies began to recruit again and warned of skills shortages.

But the upturn was short-lived. In the early 1990s unemployment was once again hovering around three million and hundreds of thousands of white collar workers in the once prosperous south east were facing joblessness for the first time. In some Continental countries the position is even worse.

It is all very bewildering — like riding on a switchback for the first time. People who have grown up with the idea that redundancy cannot happen to them are coming to terms with the fact that they are not indispensable. In the year to September 1992, over a quarter of a million executives were made compulsorily redundant, and in London and the South West of England 40 per cent of the jobless were classified as managerial staff (Labour Force Survey).

By the time this book is published one hopes the job situation will have started to improve, but it would be unwise to count the chickens before they are hatched. Instead we should try to understand the momentous changes that are taking place in the economy and society at large and prepare ourselves for whatever lies ahead.

WE CAN NEVER RECAPTURE THE PAST

Picture a social occasion where the focus of attention is an elderly

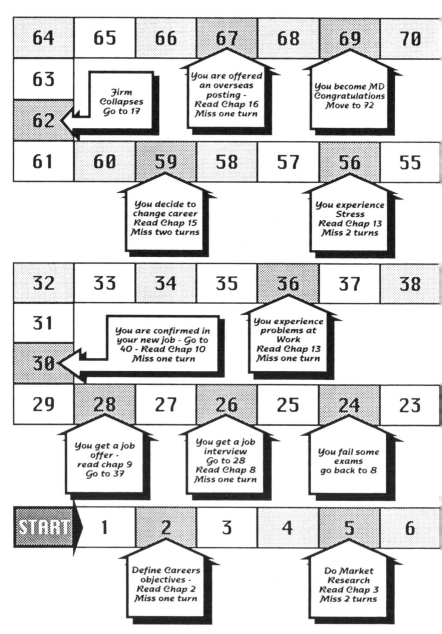

Fig. 1. Career Management Game.

Management Game

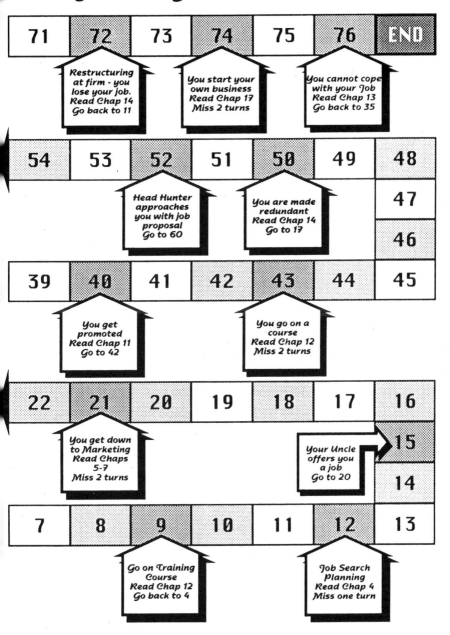

Fig. 1. Continued.

gentleman. As we draw nearer we realise that the gentleman is about
to retire, and the managing director of the firm is presenting him with
a gold watch in recognition of fifty years' service to the firm. This is
a considerable feat, and everyone is fulsome in the praise and congra-
tulations. Yet it is a feat which is unlikely to be surpassed or even
emulated in the future.

Why not? Various reasons spring to mind:

- Today an education lasts longer. The school leaving age used to
  be 14; now it is 16 and for around one third of young people in
  the UK (a greater proportion elsewhere) it is 18 or beyond.

- His firm survived unscathed. Many firms and organisations have
  changed radically over the last fifty years. They have expanded,
  contracted, merged, been taken over or gone under. Once companies such as the Rootes Group, British United Airways and
  Regent Petrol were household words. Where are they now?

- His job lasted a lifetime. When he started out it was normal to
  join an organisation and expect to remain with it until retirement
  at the age of 65. Things are different now: 'The philosophy of a
  job for life has all but disappeared and during the next 20 years
  individuals will have to become far more mobile having six or
  seven different jobs during their working lives'. [1]

The last point is particularly noteworthy. For much of the period
following the Second World War (1939-45) job security was taken for
granted. Young people joined a reputable firm or organisation — ICI
or the Civil Service, for instance — and gradually worked their way
up. You became a loyal servant of the company and in return the
company looked after your career.

Over the past 10 years the illusion of lifetime employment has
been shattered. Millions of people — both young and old — have
seen their jobs disappear overnight. Since 1984 over 200,000 mining
jobs have been lost in Britain; the number of people employed in steel
has plummeted from 230,000 to 115,000, and if you look at the car
industry in the UK you will find there are 80,000 fewer employees
than 10 years ago.

WHAT CAUSES CHANGE?

There is nothing new in this. For example, in the 18th century the woollen industry was centred on the south Cotswolds and much of the cloth was handwoven. Meanwhile up in Yorkshire an industrial revolution was taking place and with the help of machines cloth could be produced more cheaply. The Cotswold weavers refused to change their ways; as a result cheaper woollen cloth from Yorkshire displaced their handwoven products of the Cotswolds.

The moral of history is that you cannot stand in the way of 'progress' even if you regard it as a threat. It is easier to swim with the tide, and to do this you need to have access to relevant information. If you wish to swim *literally* you have to consult tidal tables; to do so *metaphorically* you need to understand how society at large is evolving.

Technical innovation

One of the major causes of change is technology, particularly information technology. Computers have all but supplanted humans in the processing of cheques and all major banks now have networks of automated teller machines to handle cash transactions. In manufacturing industry computer controlled machines are making an appearance on the shop floor, and simple repetitive tasks on assembly lines are increasingly being performed by robots.

Technology is not only changing, it is becoming better. A modern telecommunications network needs fewer engineers to service it just as better railway rolling stock requires less maintenance. Improvements in avionics mean that it only takes two pilots to fly a giant airliner, while in agriculture thanks to better fertilisers and machines Britain produces more food than it did in the 1930s with far fewer people. It is estimated that in the not too distant future a mere 10% of the population will be able to satisfy our material needs.

Global competition

Another cause of change which is linked with the first is competition. Companies and countries realise that in order to attract customers they have to provide good quality goods and services at affordable prices. If Alpha Airlines offers you steak au poivre and champagne on its flights to New York, while Zodiac Aviation serves you a stale sandwich and cold tea, it is obvious which company you will fly with. Organisations and their employees have to be better and more efficient if they are to compete in the global marketplace.

This involves cutting costs and improving productivity, and so managements are taking a hard look at how their companies and organisations are run. This often involves shortening the chain of command: why have eight levels of management when three or four will suffice? This speeds up decision making and enables organisations to respond more quickly to consumer requests. It also means more flexible work regimes: more part-timers and more staff who can work without close supervision.

If you cannot produce good quality goods and services at the right price you either go out of business or seek out a supplier who can do it for you. This has led to specialisation on a global scale. Car makers these days are essentially assembly lines where products from specialist suppliers in a number of countries are brought in to be put together. This is all possible because of improved communications. Goods and people can reach the other side of the globe in less time than it takes to drive from Lands End to John O'Groats.

Thanks to improvements in communication, not least telecommunications, national boundaries are becoming irrelevant. You can phone a colleague in New York as easily as a neighbour down the road, or he can receive a letter by fax moments after you have written it. Information is flowing faster than ever before and forcing the pace of change.

WHAT THESE CHANGES MEAN FOR YOU

By now you may be shuffling uneasily and wondering what relevance this has to this book? A great deal, in fact! None of us can divorce ourselves from the context within which we are operating and will have to operate. In this rapidly changing world we will all at times find ourselves having to run faster just to keep in the same place.

Of course, no-one can predict precisely how things will turn out. The earth could be hit by a meteor killing most of humanity and plunging the world back into the Stone Age. Alternatively we could be on the threshold of a glorious era where all nations live in harmony. The only certainty we have is that the future is uncertain. 'We live in an Age of Unreason when we can no longer assume that what worked well once will work well again, when most assumptions can legitimately be challenged.' [2]

We need to come to terms with the following ideas:

- **You cannot count any more on securing a job for life**
  Until fairly recently people in most professions did not seem to chop and change jobs all that much. It was regarded as bad form, and employers offered their workforce incentives in the form of generous pensions to persuade people to stay on. However, in the

much tougher market place of today firms have to be more responsive to consumer demand and cannot act as a refuge for time servers.

- **Your education will not end when you leave school or college**
  Because the world is changing so fast you need to equip yourself to meet new challenges, if you are not to be regarded as quaint, out of date and useless. You will need to upgrade your skills and knowledge periodically in order to keep on top of developments in your field and to compete more effectively for jobs.

- **You will need to communicate more effectively**
  We are moving towards an information based society where communication is of vital importance. (This will be dealt with at greater length elsewhere in this book). Moreover, since job moves are going to play an important role in your life you will have to learn to present yourself and your ideas to potential employers and clients as effectively as possible.

- **You may have to change career direction at least once**
  Where have all the steelmen gone — or the dockers or the miners? You have to accept the possibility that one day your job too will cease to exist, or else it will lose its appeal and become a chore. The good news is that as some jobs disappear, new ones take their place. There is no sense in clinging to a sinking raft; you have to be prepared for the eventuality of a career change at some time in the future — perhaps a drastic one.

Changing trades and professions
Look at the following list of trades and professions.

bank clerk	printer
car mechanic	secretary/typist
doctor	social worker
pilot	teacher
politician	train driver

Try to identify

- which ones will disappear before the year 2050
- which ones will exist more or less unchanged
- which ones will still be around but virtually unrecognisable?

Now turn to the Appendix on page 177 and compare your ideas with those that are set out there.

Managing your career

Living as we do in a restless age in which nothing stands still for very long it is essential to chart a path through the maze. It is no use hoping that the winds of fortune will blow you on to the right track.

Careers need to be *planned*. At one time this would have meant sitting down and deciding what sort of position you expect to hold in a particular firm in five, ten or twenty years' time. This is no longer an option in a time of change. No-one can predict with any certainty that these positions will still exist: they could disappear in a restructuring exercise, or the organisation itself may disappear.

The trouble is people never start to think about career planning until they meet with some kind of crisis when the mind is not at its clearest. A person who has just been made redundant is unlikely to be able to sit back reflectively and take a long-term view of his future. As a consequence, short-term solutions are sought, which may not prove satisfactory in the long run.

Planning your career requires you to analyse the changes that are happening around you and make decisions as to how to deal with these circumstances. It also means you need to look ahead, set objectives, and then work out strategies which will enable you to achieve your goals.

In a 'job for life' organisation this was often done for you through regular staff appraisals which offer feedback on your performance and enable decisions to be made on the future direction of your career — promotion, further training or redeployment.

But an increasing number of jobs nowadays are on fixed term contracts or else carry no guarantee of promotion, as organisations seek greater flexibility. Even apparently permanent positions are unlikely to last for ever. You have to face up to the fact that your career is your own responsibility and you cannot expect anyone else to manage it for you.

CASE STUDIES

It is now time for you to meet five people who will be with us throughout the book. They all need to get to grips with managing their careers, and here we will discover why.

Angela, the sixth former

Angela is a sixth former faced with a number of crucial decisions, one of which she has to make during the next few weeks: whether to start work when she leaves school or whether to go on to higher education. If she decides on the latter course of action she has to decide what subjects to study and where to study them and submit an application with all due speed.

It is never too soon to start thinking about the future. The trouble with Angela is that she is only thinking about her next move, not about her ultimate objective. First she needs to establish her career aims and then work out a strategy for achieving them. Once she has done this the next move will fall into place.

Bob, a recent graduate

Bob is a recent graduate. After several months spent applying for jobs and getting nowhere, he has just landed a management trainee-ship with a firm in the City, but he has come to the sad conclusion that he is not cut out for this kind of thing. Should he go ahead regardless?

Bob's problem is that he has not mapped out his future. At university he dedicated all his time to his chosen subject and to having a reasonable social life. He failed to look beyond his immediate goal of attaining a degree. It is a complete anti-climax if, having studied a subject he enjoyed and was good at, he now has to settle for a job he is not cut out for.

It is essential for Bob to investigate the range of possibilities open to him and work out a plan of attack before the doors of opportunity start closing. Some already have.

Colin — 'thirty-something'

To all intents and purposes thirty-one year old Colin is a success. He joined his firm XYZ Ltd immediately he left college and has been with them ever since. He has just got married and has a nice-looking house in a leafy suburb and in due course his wife will give up her job to concentrate on bringing up a family.

Colin's problem is that his experience is limited to one firm and he is now on autopilot. He is at an age when he should be looking out for new challenges, and if XYZ is not offering them it could be time to move on. You can, after all, stay with one organisation so long that you get taken for granted, and when you really need to leave it becomes difficult to sever links.

Colin is a much sought after employee if he only realised it. Firms are keen to recruit people who are still in the first flush of youth but have several years of good solid experience behind them. This would be a good time to make an upward move, but he needs to define his career aims first of all.

Doreen, a married 'returner'

Doreen is forty. She has spent the past fifteen years as a housewife and mother, but the time is coming when her children will be grown up and the family roost will feel eerily quiet. Before she got married she worked as a secretary, but she now feels she would stand little chance of landing a similar post today as bosses prefer bright young things.

Doreen is an intelligent woman of considerable talent who would be wasted in a dead end job. She has at least twenty years of active working life ahead of her and there is no reason why she should not be able eventually to get an interesting and worthwhile job. However, the way back into the workplace for so-called 'returners' is not always easy. Doreen needs to plan her return with care.

Edward at fifty

Edward is fifty and feels somewhat vulnerable. The organisation for which he works has started to slim down its workforce — they call it 'down-sizing'. He fears that in a year or two some of the more senior staff, of which he is one, will be offered what is euphemistically called early retirement — which he dreads. In the meantime he is content to soldier on hoping for the best.

Edward is in excellent health and a person who has a wide range of abilities not all of which have been properly exploited. He can look forward to another twenty-five years — perhaps longer if he keeps himself fit, and for a person in his shoes this could be a time of self-fulfilment rather than a winding down period.

His financial commitments are easing off; he has virtually paid off his mortgage, he no longer has a family to support, and his savings amount to a tidy sum. A lot of doors are now closed to him, but if he plans his strategy carefully and is persistent, he could find himself taking on a new lease of life.

[1]   Malcolm McKee, 'Why we need a pensions framework for the future' in *The Family Magazine*, Autumn 1994.

[2]   Charles Handy, *The Age of Unreason* (Business Books 1989).

2
Defining Your Career Objectives

Some people regard work as a curse rather than a blessing, but when it comes to the crunch few of us would swap a busy day at the workplace for a life of non-stop leisure. It is not difficult to understand why. Work gives us a purpose in life and helps define who and what we are.

You may grumble that your job is tedious and miserable but that does not invalidate the statement; it simply means that you are in the wrong job and you need to move on to something more in tune with your needs. The purpose of this book is to help you to achieve this goal.

There is no doubt that you will be better doing a job you like rather than one that is uncongenial. Not that every job offers hours of uninterrupted pleasure; there are moments of tedium and stress in any work, but with luck the advantages will more than make up for the drawbacks.

CLARIFYING YOUR AIMS

What do you look for in a job?
Let us start by getting down to basics. Job expectations differ from person to person and you need to consider what you want from a particular job or your career as a whole. Look at the following items — which ones reflect your aspirations?

- **Achievement**. You want to face challenges and achieve results.

- **Autonomy**. You are keen to work independently of others.

- **High earnings**. A good salary will enable you and your family to enjoy a high standard of living.

- **Outdoor life**. You would like a job where you spend a large part of your time out of doors.

21

- **Responsibility**. You are keen to take responsibility and possibly seek a job where you can exercise leadership.

- **Security**. You want a secure job with an organisation which will look after you well.

- **Self-development**. You are keen to acquire different skills and advance in your career.

- **Self-expression**. You need opportunities to be creative and use your personality to good effect.

- **Social relevance**. You want the opportunity to meet with and help other people.

- **Status**. You would like a high profile position which affords you a good deal of prestige.

- **Variety**. You seek the chance to use a range of skills within a variety of contexts.

This list makes no claim to be definitive and you may well discover you have other motives as well.

What do others look for in a job?

Some time ago the Henley Forecasting Centre polled some managers on their attitudes to work. Look at the following and rank them in order of importance to you and then consider how this would compare with the preferences of the managers.

Factor	*Rating 1 to 6*
Amount you earn	_____
Doing a job you know people respect	_____
Having a variety of things to do	_____
Using knowledge and experience to make decisions	_____
Being with and making friends	_____
Having control over what you do	_____

For the Henley results turn to page 178.

How your circumstances may affect your requirements

Your personal circumstances at a given moment could affect the kind of career you decide to pursue. Someone with heavy financial commitments, for instance, may put high earnings at the top of the list; fifty year olds will probably attach greater importance to job security than people at the start of their careers.

If you are already comfortably off, you may look on work as an extension of your own interests and will pay less regard to the financial benefits offered by a particular post. And if you belong to a family of high achievers, your prime motivation may well be to rise to the top of a poorly paid but prestigious profession rather than become a millionaire.

There are others for whom the actual job takes second place to other interests, such as parenthood. You may decide to play a leading role in public life — by becoming a borough councillor or a JP, for instance; or you may wish to develop your talents as a musician or sportsman. In all such cases you need an employer who is prepared to be flexible and you may be unable to expend the effort and extra time necessary to propel you to a job at the top.

If you live in an area of high unemployment and are in no position to move, you may have to settle for second best — for the time being, at least. Domestic considerations can also loom large; a working mother, for instance, may be unwilling to take on more responsibility if it means working long and irregular hours; and in dual income families one partner may have to sacrifice promotion prospects for the sake of the other.

So you may have to temper your aspirations a little and make sure that your goals are realistic and within your reach. The more you consider, the more you may become aware of obstacles in your path, but remember, most impediments look more awesome than they really are. Let us consider some of them.

OVERCOMING THE BARRIERS

The American entertainer Sammy Davies Jnr suffered from a number of disadvantages. He was small, black, and Jewish; he had only one eye and was not particularly good looking; yet that did not stop him from becoming a great Hollywood star. Dr Stephen Hawking is paralysed and confined to a wheel chair, but despite tremendous communication difficulties he has written that monumental work, *A Brief History of Time*, and holds down a Professorship of Mathematics at Cambridge University.

The following items are frequently cited as handicaps, but with proper career management they can usually be overcome.

Overcoming poor education

Although you occasionally hear of illiterate people who have gone on to become millionaires, generally speaking a good education gives you the best start in life. If you have missed out on your education in the past, there are ways of remedying the situation. The range of educational opportunities has never been greater in the UK and if full-time education is beyond your reach you could explore the various part-time flexible learning schemes that are available. For further details turn to Chapter 12.

Overcoming physical handicap

Some jobs require able-bodied people, but in today's knowledge-based economy, jobs that involve manipulating data are more numerous than those requiring physical strength. This means that capable people with disabilities have a much wider range of occupations to choose from than they may realise. In addition, organisations in the UK are encouraged to employ disabled people with the provision of government grants to adapt their premises and equipment.

Overcoming sex/gender prejudice

In the past women were discriminated against in the promotion stakes, but attitudes are changing thanks partly to changes in the law and in the world of work. There is evidence to suggest that in expanding knowledge-based industries women with a good education can more than hold their own. Moreover the proportion of women in the labour force is projected to increase.

Yet many married women are faced with a dilemma at a crucial stage in their lives: whether to concentrate on their career or bringing up their families — which is, of course, a career in itself. The introduction of workplace crèches, job sharing and more flexible working arrangements now make it easier to manage both.

Overcoming social background

The influence of the old school tie is declining fast, and in most walks of life ability now counts for more than social connections. Increasingly company board rooms are populated not by Old Etonians but by people with regional accents who have come up through the state sector of education. Rather than gaze enviously at those better off than yourself, set yourself goals; take advantage of the education and training opportunities which will help you attain these goals. If shortage of cash is a problem, you may be eligible for grants, bursaries or loans.

Succeeding from an ethnic minority

People from ethnic minorities may feel they suffer from a disadvantage when applying for jobs because of racial prejudice. While racial prejudice may not have been eliminated in the UK, most self-respecting firms and public sector bodies operate staffing policies which purport to be non-discriminatory, and if their workforce remains overwhelmingly white the reason could be that relatively few people from an ethnic minority actually apply.

In some cases people from ethnic minorities fail to make the grade because they are poorly or inappropriately qualified — not for racial reasons. However, thanks to the importance many minorities place on their children's education many second generation immigrants to the UK are achieving higher examination grades than their indigenous counterparts. In areas where ability counts people from ethnic minorities really can make it to the top whatever the colour of their skin.

No doubt you can think of other obstacles — family problems, financial difficulties, time constraints, and so on; but if you examine them carefully you may well find they are little more than figments of the imagination or — at most — temporary impediments which will eventually pass. To manage your career successfully you need to think positively. Obstacles are there to be overcome.

WORKING OUT A STRATEGY

Once a manager in an organisation has identified objectives he has to work out a strategy which will enable the organisation to achieve them. He does this by taking account of his current resources and planning how to mobilise them.

Take a leaf out of his book when managing your career. Remember, unless you are extraordinarily lucky you will not achieve your goal in a single leap. Instead you have to plot your progress step by step. This applies just as much to a person in mid-career who is keen to branch out in a new direction, as to a school leaver.

Step 1: seek out relevant information

It is sensible to find out as much as possible about your destination, before you embark on your journey. There is a wealth of information about different jobs and careers in many reference libraries and from various trade and professional associations. (See Bibliography.) While a good many of the careers books are written with young people in mind, the advice they offer would benefit a person of any age. If possible, you should also seek out people in the business who can show you what the work entails.

Step 2: establish a shortlist of realistic options

Having obtained details of the various careers of interest to you, you may find some that you can exclude. For instance, it is difficult to enter certain professions once you are past a certain age; others have stringent entry requirements which may be hard to meet. Some professions are overcrowded; others are in decline. You need to pick a career with a future and in which you stand a reasonable chance of success. (See **Researching your market**.)

Step 3: acquire the right qualifications and training

Having a few letters after your name is no guarantee you are anything more than merely competent at your job, but good qualifications can sway the balance in your favour, even more so if they are particularly relevant to a particular position or task. Ideally, work out your career objectives first, and *then* choose which subjects you will study — rather than vice versa, as is often the case.

Step 4: gain relevant experience

Qualifications need to be backed up by worthwhile experience if you are to progress in your career. Some courses have a substantial practical content — perhaps even with 'on the job' experience. Others tend to be theoretical. Both 'general' experience (*ie* experience of the workaday world) and experience specific to your field (*eg* how to drill a tooth, how to draw up accounts) are necessary.

Step 5: embarking on your career (or new career)

This involves presenting yourself to employers and clients, persuading them that you are the right person for the job, and subsequently getting to grips with the job itself, understanding what is required of you and establishing a reputation for yourself as a credible, competent and trustworthy professional.

CASE STUDIES

Angela — a career in public service?
Angela is keen to embark on a career which offers her opportunities for self expression and has an element of social relevance. Social work, teaching, the police — she has not yet decided on her career. Angela ought to spend time in her school careers library reading up on the various possibilities and perhaps going on a work experience scheme organised by the local careers office. It would be good if she could come to a decision soon, as this will influence her choice of course in the future.

Bob seeks variety and challenge
Bob is keen to use his creative talents on a variety of tasks. He has not really worked out his career plans and although his arts degree marks him out as a person of intellect, he is not sure where it may lead him. He applied for a management trainee position with a multi-national firm on impulse, but is now having second thoughts. Yet a bird in hand is worth two in a bush, and the experience would be useful — not least in building up his credibility in the eyes of employers. It is a first career step but not an irrevocable one.

Colin wants to move ahead
For Colin high earnings, responsibility and status are important. He notes that some of his close contemporaries are earning more than he is, and a few now have very high-powered jobs. This is a good time for him to reassess his career aims and work out a strategy which will set him on course again. This might entail upgrading his qualifications and perhaps moving on to another job.

Doreen's confidence problem
Doreen is a caring sort of person; she seeks a career with social relevance and offering an element of security. However, she has not worked for a company or organisation for a good many years and feels she has little to offer potential employers. In fact, there is no reason why she should not ultimately land a very interesting job, but

she has to plan her reentry into the workforce with care. This could involve taking a course — perhaps on a part-time basis.

Edward rethinks at fifty

Edward is fairly well off, so high earnings are less important than they once were. He feels his job is under threat and if pushed he would not be averse to finding work offering greater scope for self expression. He wonders whether he has left it too late to go through the rigmarole of setting himself new career goals. In fact, his fiftieth birthday is an excellent time to reassess his current objectives which may have changed a good deal over the years. Edward now in the prime of life when he could achieve a number of ambitions as yet unfulfilled, some of which could involve branching off in new directions. But to be successful in this he must first define his objectives.

3
Researching Your Market

LIVING IN A MARKET-BASED ECONOMY

During the course of your career you will face lots of situations where you have to choose between different courses of action. Some of the decisions will be difficult, and have far reaching repercussions on your subsequent career, hence the importance of making every effort to get them right.

One cannot just trust to luck in today's world. The road to ruin is paved with gambles that just did not come off. To make effective, sensible decisions you need to be well informed.

It is easy to be wise after the event. With the benefit of hindsight many wars could have been avoided and catastrophes averted. In the fields of commerce and industry there are countless stories of products which have been put on the market and failed to find any buyers, resulting in substantial losses for the companies concerned.

This is why any sensible firm will invest time and effort in market research. By obtaining information about who their potential clients are, where they are and what they want, they can minimise the risks involved in launching a new product.

Market research is not, however, confined to industry and commerce. Government departments and local authorities, too, make use of market research techniques on anything from public transport to housing. Without reliable information of this nature officials are working in the dark and any policies they come up with risk being flawed.

LEARNING HOW TO MARKET YOURSELF

If commerce and government find market research a useful tool in formulating their plans, why not individuals? After all, we now live in the information age; the well informed person or organisation will always have the edge over those that are not.

In order to manage your career effectively in a rapidly changing world you need to have the best available information on employment prospects. Few people can afford the services of a market research company (though some careers consultants claim to do market research of behalf of their clients).

The alternative is to do the research yourself. This will involve collecting information on jobs in your particular discipline, analysing it and interpreting it. Systematic research like this should identify those areas of the job market you need to concentrate on.

If you can get a clear idea from the outset as to who is recruiting, where the jobs are and what kind of skills are required, then you will be able to target your applications very effectively.

Tracking down information

A good starting point for your research might be the periodicals room of your local library. Here you will need to:

● take a look at the job ad columns and check how many jobs there are on offer in your particular field (or fields)

● take note of the qualifications and personal attributes that are being demanded

● note what salaries are being proposed, and try to relate these to your financial needs

● check which companies and organisations are currently looking for staff.

This investigation should enable you to get a 'feel' for the market. It would also be worth your while to note down addresses, phone and fax numbers of organisations you may want to contact in the future.

You may be lucky and find that there are plenty of opportunities in the careers that appear in your 'shortlist'. On the other hand, there may appear to be very few openings at all.

However, things may not be as bad as they seem. Some kinds of jobs are rarely advertised while others are only advertised in the specialist press. At certain times of the year recruitment advertising tends to fall off: few vacancies are advertised around Christmas, for example.

Don't just concentrate on the job pages and ignore the rest of

the newspaper or journal. If you do, you could miss vital information.
Read the business pages too, in order to find out which firms and sectors of the economy are expanding.

● Look at articles on careers and employment matters, such as those that appear in the Appointments Section of *The Times* and the various careers publications (see Bibliography).

● Delve into more publications specialising in your field of expertise *(eg Nursing Times, Construction News, Computer Weekly).*

● Read relevant articles in the various job annuals *(eg Directory of Opportunities for Graduates).*

So far you have concentrated on what market researchers call **desk research**. But you need also to do a little **qualitative research** as well. This involves seeking out people who can offer you an insight into the jobs market. These might include:

● personnel officers
● employment agencies
● recruitment specialists
● business contacts
● careers officers
● colleagues who have a talent for keeping their ear to the ground.

Gather as much material as you can and then try to decide how you fit into the pattern of things. What are the current prospects in the career areas in which you are interested? Have you the sort of qualifications and skills that employers want?

Do you have transferable skills?
Newly fledged graduates often feel that their qualifications are their main selling point, but employers are looking for a good deal more than this.
Here is a list of qualities that a leading British engineering firm expects its graduate recruits to have. Rank these according to importance and compare your rankings with those on page 179. There may be some surprises.

Quality	*Ranking (1 to 10)*
numeracy	_____
communication skills	_____
ability to work as part of a team	_____
problem solving skills	_____
analytical skills	_____
flexibility	_____
adaptability	_____
intra-personal skills	_____
decision making skills	_____
ability to make independent judgements	_____

Some of these are classed as **transferable skills**, *ie* skills that can be used in a wide range of jobs. Often people (including arts graduates) are let down by their poor communication skills. These skills would include:

● report writing
● presenting a case
● chairing a meeting
● offering advice
● seeking information from libraries and databases
● writing memos.

Whatever your chosen field, skills like these will prove a tremendous asset, and it would be sensible to develop expertise in these areas if you have not done so already.

Matching yourself to the market

Investigating the market will inject an element of realism into your thinking. You should now be aware of the job preferences on your short list which are non-starters (*eg* because of inappropriate qualifications, age restrictions, diminishing prospects) and those which offer a promising future.

You need to consider the qualifications, skills and experience that you can offer. For a younger person qualifications will be the things that matter most; for a job changer the latter two may be of greater importance. And yet these are the details that we are least sure of.

Before any matching can take place you need to identify what skills and experience you have. Disregard any job titles you may have had or subjects you have studied. Instead, concentrate on past activities and areas of expertise which you can draw on and apply successfully in a variety of contexts. The *Management Self Assessment System* may be of assistance.

Written tests
Some of these abilities can be measured by written tests:

- verbal ability — good with words, able to communicate well
- numerical ability
- perceptual ability — able to make sense of abstract information
- spatial ability — able to visualise 3D objects from drawings and diagrams
- technical ability
- acuity — ability to do routine tasks quickly and with great accuracy
- analytical ability — able to solve problems.

There are various tests designed to assess personality and attitude, but we can disregard these for the moment. See how good you are at assessing yourself.

Assessing yourself
For a start list the things you have done — in school, in college, at the workplace and in private life — and the skills you have used for each. Which things do you do particularly well? What achievements are you particularly proud of?

Do not be critical or dwell on your shortcomings or failures. Your assessment has to be positive and concentrate on your strengths — those qualities which sooner or later you are going to have to sell.

Sell? — yes, because this is what marketing is all about. Having analysed the results of your market research, you have to tailor your offering (*ie* yourself) to the needs of your customer (the employer). However, before you can recommend yourself to a client you need to know what you are selling.

Forget about job titles or qualifications for the moment. Instead, be prepared to sell your particular skills and unique personality.

'O wad some Pow'r the giftie gie us
To see oursels as ithers see us!
It wad frae mony a blunder free us
And foolish notion.' [1]

Robert Burns has a point here. If you have problems in uncovering your special qualities, then enlist the help of your close intimates who may see strengths in you of which you are unaware. The following checklist, which some selectors use, may help to concentrate the mind.

● Impact on others: what impression do you make on people you meet?

● Qualifications and experience: how does what you have already done equip you for the future?

● Emotional adjustment: how do you get on with other people? How do you behave when the going gets tough?

● Motivation: how enthusiastic are you about your work? How well are you able to motivate others?

● Innate abilities: what skills come naturally to you?

Play around with different ideas, brainstorm a little. Make a list of the jobs — however improbable — that you could at least make a stab at. Don't be ashamed to fantasize, for marketing is an activity which requires creative thinking.

It also requires something else. As one senior executive writes: 'The only difference between those who made it and those who didn't was one quality. It had nothing to do with talent, connections, academic qualifications or interpersonal skills. Those who made it simply possessed more perseverance than those who did not.'

CASE STUDIES

Angela uses local research facilities

Angela is much better placed to research the market than she realises. She and her teachers will have access to the facilities of either the local authority careers service or the Independent Schools Careers Organisation (ISCO). There are a number of attractively presented careers publications for young people which offer up to date information on different careers. They include *Springboard, Careerscope* and *School Leaver*. Angela really ought to dip into these.

Bob gets help through college

Bob also has access to a good deal of information from his college careers advisory service. He is entitled to use this service even after graduation. The Association of Graduate Careers Advisory Services (AGCAS) monitors graduate employment and Bob's local careers advisor should be able to give him a good picture of the current state of the graduate jobs market. There are a number of useful magazines and newspapers which contain articles on graduate careers. They include *Graduate Careers, Graduate Post, Current Vacancies* and *Science & Technology Graduate.*

Colin checks his professional body

Colin should have plenty of contacts who can keep him abreast of developments in his own field. His professional association is a useful source of information, and regular perusal of the press specialising in his particular field should keep him up to date. Colin's main problem is that he identifies too closely with his job title, and this restricts the range of other options he could otherwise consider.

Doreen isn't sure how to start

Doreen feels out on a limb. If you are starting again from scratch where can you find out about the state of the jobs market? The local careers service might be a possibility: its facilities extend to everybody and not just school leavers. The National Advisory Centre on Careers for Women or the Career Development Centre may be able to put Doreen on the right track, and there may be local initiatives designed to help women back into work. The magazine *Returners* offers up-to-date careers articles for women in Doreen's position.

Edward needs to make new contacts

Edward, like Colin, has access to a wide range of data about his profession if he cares to read it. However, this will be of only limited use to him if he decides to change career. Perhaps he should consult some of the contacts he has made outside his own profession, for example in the local Rotary Club or Railway Preservation Society of which he is a member. A subscription to *Escape*, a magazine for career changers, may be a help.

[1]   *To a Louse*, Robert Burns.

4
Planning Your Job Search

Having used market research to identify the areas on which to concentrate, it is now time to leap into action. If you are a job seeker or job changer you need to seek suitable positions to apply for. If you decide to opt for self-employment you will be formulating your marketing plans and be on the lookout for clients.

Job seeking has become a little more sophisticated since the days of Dick Whittington who set off from his Gloucestershire village to find fame and fortune in London. His 20th century successor is less likely to tramp the streets of London asking people for a job. Newspapers, recruitment agencies and executive search consultants have become important players in the job finding game.

JOB ADS

Making sense of job advertisements

For a great many people the first step towards a new position is an advertisement in a newspaper or magazine. Some are big, some look insignificant — but all are worthy of attention. However:

- Not all job adverts are what they seem, so it helps if you can read between the lines. For instance, the organisation which has initiated the announcement may not have a vacancy, but simply wants to test the market for people with that kind of expertise.

- In other cases the vacancy could well have been filled before the details appeared in the press. Local authorities, for example, often prefer the devil they know to an outsider when it comes to making an appointment, but their regulations often insist that vacancies at a certain level are advertised.

It may seem grossly unfair that a candidate from inside an institution should have a headstart over other candidates who may be better qualified. But once you manage to get inside that charmed circle you will probably see matters in a completely different light.

When you see a post — particularly a senior post — advertised, consider for a moment *why* it has appeared in the paper. If a company is expanding, then the vacancy is probably quite genuine. If an organisation is facing a shortage of expertise in certain skills, there is no reason to doubt its authenticity. Or if a firm has a deliberate policy of recruiting outsiders, you need have no qualms, though it may be harder to determine this fact.

Recruitment can be a costly business, so the smaller the firm the less likely it is that its advertisements will be large and expensive. There is no need to feel that the biggest advertisements are necessarily the most genuine or offer the best opportunities.

If the 'impressive' advertisement has been placed by the company itself be prepared for a certain amount of hype and unwitting misinformation. The epithet 'well-established' for example could point to a conservatively led company which has seen better days. If they are offering 'an exceptional opportunity to the right person' it could mean that they want someone who will not rock an already leaking boat.

At the other end of the scale, the 'young, dynamic hi-tech company' in need of 'an experienced accountant' might well turn out to be headed by a group of unworldly boffins who have got themselves into an unholy financial mess. And the company which regards itself as 'exciting, progressive and ambitious' which requires 'experienced and motivated graduates in their early twenties' is clearly out of touch with reality.

To check out your guesswork, get hold of past reports and other literature relating to the firm to which you intend to apply. If you are in doubt as to whether you would fit into the general scheme of things there is no harm in sending off for an application form and further details (including the most recent annual report).

You may find that advertisements drafted by intermediaries (*ie* recruitment consultants) are a good deal more informative and useful. Outside consultants have the advantage of objectivity both with regard to the post on offer and the firm itself. And since their function is to communicate their clients' requirements effectively, to attract suitable applicants, they make sure that the information they put out is factual and reliable.

Recurrent advertisements

What are you to make of the job which is readvertised after you have applied for it and possibly been turned down? There could be a number of reasons for this. Apart from the obvious one — that the selectors have not been impressed by any of the candidates — the appointee may have withdrawn at the last moment, or the organisation may have decided to revise the terms of reference for the post. At worst, some hapless junior clerk may have put all the applications through the shredder by mistake. Everything is possible — even in the best regulated offices.

The recurrent advertisement could signify a number of things. Aside from 'testing the market', it could reveal something more sinister. Perhaps the organisation has difficulty in recruiting or retaining staff, in which case further investigation is called for.

Are they simply bad employers offering poor pay and uncongenial working conditions, or are they having difficulty in recruiting enough staff because of skills shortages? In certain professions there is traditionally a high drop-out rate, and this is why papers are always awash with adverts for sales staff.

Methods by which companies recruit staff

Advertisements in regional press	87%
Advertisements in specialist press	80%
Advertisements in national press	78%
Job Centres	71%
Employment agencies	62%
Recruitment consultants	61%
Executive search consultants (Headhunters)	36%
Career conventions	35%
Open days	32%
Recruitment fairs	32%
University 'milk rounds'	21%
Radio advertising	17%
Other forms of recruitment	6%

IPM Survey 1989.

USING INTERMEDIARIES

As the accompanying chart shows, employers do not rely only on advertising to recruit staff. They employ intermediaries, such as recruitment consultants, employment agencies, headhunters — call them what you will. These are recruitment specialists, whose job it is to find people who will match the needs of their clients.

It is not unusual for intermediaries to advertise positions on behalf of their clients, especially for high ranking jobs. However, if they already have a good selection of people on their files, this may prove unnecessary. It therefore makes sense to approach several agencies with a view to getting on their books.

A personal visit can work wonders. If you manage to catch a consultant at a quiet time, he or she will probably be willing to talk to you at length in order to learn as much as possible about you. Apart from giving you information on the state of the market for your trade or profession, he might be willing to suggest other agencies that are better placed to help you.

Some agencies handle general vacancies while others tend to specialise in certain fields (*eg* accountancy, nursing, computers), though this is not always evident from their names. Display advertisements in Yellow Pages often supply information of this nature, and the *Yearbook of Recruitment and Employment Services* classifies its members according to specialism. *The Executive Grapevine* lists the activities of consultants which recruit for managerial positions.

Choosing an employment agency

Which of the following recruitment agencies would you go to if you wanted a job in one of the job sectors mentioned below? (Most are members of the Federation of Recruitment and Employment Services.)

Agency	*Job sector*
Anders Glaser Wills	_____
Astron	_____
James Baker	_____
BNA	_____
Gabbitas Truman & Thring	_____
Harrison Willis	_____
Job Centre	_____
Quarry Dougall	_____
Travail	_____
Universal Aunts	_____
VIP Recruitment	_____

Accountancy, domestic work, engineering, hotels and catering, IT, legal work, overseas jobs, publishing, nursing, teaching, temporary work, secretarial work.

Compare your answers with those on page 179.

How agencies operate

Recruitment agencies in the UK derive their income from employers; British law prevents them from charging job applicants a fee, even in the case of jobs overseas. So their primary aim is *not* to find you a job, but to fill their clients' vacancies. If you hear nothing from an agency, there is no point in making a complaint.

However, most recruitment consultants are courteous and helpful to job applicants. They have to be — otherwise they would not have any good quality candidates to recommend to their clients. You should show them similar courtesy by keeping them informed of your movements, especially when you have landed a job.

If you are a high flier in a senior position, do not be surprised if you receive an approach from out of the blue to see if you are interested in moving on. This is an indication that you are being 'headhunted': an **executive search** consultant is following your career with interest. Executive search is the top end of the recruitment consultancy business, and if you respond positively to such an approach, you could well receive a number of attractive job proposals in due course.

None of these organisations should be confused with **outplacement consultants**. These are organisations which are called in when a firm is making staff redundant to help the affected staff to find new jobs. (See also Chapters 14 and 15.)

TAKING THE INITIATIVE: THE CREATIVE JOB SEARCH

Approaching recruitment agencies is a more proactive method of securing employment, sometimes known as the speculative approach. Rather than using some intermediaries you make direct contact with employers.

This can be something of a hit or miss exercise unless you target your applications carefully. You have probably already identified some relevant ones during your market research exercise. If not, ask around. One American job-hunting manual suggests you call in to see the mayor of the locality where you wish to work in order to gain information on employment prospects.

While the mayor of the average borough in the UK might seem the last person to advise you on such matters, there are other people who are better placed to do so including:

- local chambers of commerce
- trade union representatives
- your professional association.

Do not hesitate to make full use of your network of contacts. It has been suggested that 75% of jobs are filled this way. The contacts would include:

- relations
- friends
- business or college acquaintances
- teachers and lecturers
- former employers.

Educational institutions, particularly local colleges which maintain close links with business and industry, are often a useful source of information on jobs provided you make the right contacts. Careers advisory services usually have reference rooms where you can peruse vacancy notices and bulletins, and you may be able to chat to someone — even if you have no links with that particular establishment.

Large organisations often prefer to recruit in-house and publicise vacancies in their house journals and on staff notice boards. It is useful if you can 'infiltrate' these by asking friends who work there to keep their eyes open on your behalf and to pass on information on suitable job openings.

Reference books are another source of information. Many trades and professions publish annual directories *(eg The Bankers Almanac & Year Book, The Chemical Industry Directory)* which list the organisations operating in that particular field. The *Kompass Register of British Industry & Commerce British Companies Index* (Moodies Services), *Guide to Key British Enterprises* (Dun and Bradstreet) and *The Times 100 Leading Companies* (Times Newspapers Ltd – annual) all contain a wealth of information on all sectors.

Once you have established a list of organisations that you believe could make use of your skills, you can send off speculative letters. (See next chapter.) The principal object is to find out about a vacancy before it is advertised — to be ahead of the crowd, in other words. Indeed, if you play your cards right, the management may decide to dispense with the trouble and expense of a recruitment advertisement because you fit the bill perfectly.

Even better, you may be able to persuade an employer to create a job especially for you. It sometimes happens, but unless the employee happens to be a doting relative or you manage to be in exactly the right place at the right time, you will need to have exceptional powers of persuasion.

If properly done the speculative approach can prove rewarding. Although we have come a long way since the days of Dick Whittington, there is still much to be said for going out and actively seeking a position rather than just waiting for a job advertisement.

CASE STUDIES

Angela starts with the local paper

If Angela decides to go straight into a job when she leaves school, the first place she is likely to look is her local newspaper which usually carries a good range of job advertisements for junior posts. There are however other routes to a job. Many schools and careers services have links with local firms and may be able to arrange for her to visit some of them and talk things over; or she might make contact with employers at a careers fair; or there is Uncle Quentin who works for a large insurance company and has offered to put in a good word for her.

Bob and the 'milk round'

Bob landed his first job by making contact with his prospective employer at a graduate jobs fair. These events bring together a large number of players, and are normally staged in the late summer and autumn. Some of his friends got fixed up earlier in the year when a group of company recruiters visited his college on a recruitment tour of different campuses, commonly known as the 'milk round'. However, Bob could also have responded to advertisements in the press, including the graduate jobs papers mentioned in the last chapter, or approached one of the employers mentioned in *DOG*.

Colin puts out feelers

There are lots of advertisements in newspapers and professional journals for qualified and experienced personnel in Colin's age range. Some of the positions appeal to him. However, he should also register with a few executive recruitment consultancies which will forward his name and particulars to their clients when specific vacancies arise.

Colin should also use his network of contacts, especially business contacts, who know his capabilities and may be willing to help him further his career. Finally, he could explore opportunities within his own firm, particularly if it is strongly committed to management development.

Doreen gets networking

Doreen, alas, finds few advertisements in newspapers for women of her age, and most of those are for low paid, undemanding jobs. She may fare better if she registers with an employment agency. Some of these are used to dealing with women returners and might be able to slot her into a few temporary jobs at first to enable her to build up her self-confidence and credibility with employers. The careers service may be able to give her a few leads, and she should make use of her network of contacts.

Edward's wide range of contacts

Edward is distressed to find that virtually every job advertisement he sees excludes candidates over the age of 40, though this does not necessarily mean that nobody over that age is being recruited. His best plan is to adopt a speculative approach. In particular he should make use of his wide range of contacts, including the professional association of which he is a member. He also ought to get onto the books of a few executive recruitment agencies, which he can find listed in *The Executive Grapevine*, and start investigating self-employment opportunities.

SPECIALIST RECRUITMENT ADVERTISING CALENDAR

	Guardian	*Independent*	*Times*
Monday	Creative Media Secretarial	Engineering Technology IT	Education Secretarial
Tuesday	Education	Financial Secretarial	Public Sector Technology Legal
Wednesday	Public Sector Social Services	Media Marketing	Media Marketing Secretarial General
Thursday	Business Finance Computing	Education Public Sector General	Financial Secretarial General Banking
Friday	Housing Leisure Science Technology Conservation	Legal	
Saturday	General		

Fig. 2. Specialist recruitment advertising calendar.

5
Marketing Yourself by Letter

If you are looking for a job, aiming for promotion or seeking out clients you will not make much progress if you hide your light under a bushel. Be ready to present yourself effectively to potential employers and clients — either in person, in writing or on the telephone.

First class presentation is crucial right from the very first contact. The sad fact is that if you do not make a favourable impact from the start, you may never get another bite of the cherry. Somehow you have to make yourself sound exciting, dynamic and irresistible to the person on the receiving end.

Think of those mail shots which arrive through the post every morning citing the advantages of this and persuading you to buy that. The organisations that despatch these by the million are seeking to grab your attention. This is the first shot in what they hope will become a long and rewarding relationship.

HOW TO MAKE CONTACT

Applying for a job — or angling for a contract — is a form of sales activity. We live in a competitive age when firms are often inundated with applications and can be quite choosy as to whom they employ.

Have you bought or borrowed any books lately? If so, try to remember which of the following items attracted you to that particular book:

- the author
- recommendation by a friend
- a good review
- the title
- the cover
- the blurb.

In the case of a purchase on impulse the last two factors may have had a particular influence.

Although publishing is sometimes looked upon as a rather exalted profession, publishers are really in the business of selling their books rather than airing new literary talents.

The pictures on the dust covers are designed to attract your attention while the publisher's blurb is designed — not so much to inform you about the book — but to stimulate you to want desperately to read it.

Your first magnum opus — your initial letter — must take a leaf out of the publisher's inventory of selling skills. The letter has to engage the attention of the recipient right from the outset. Make the selector want to meet you.

MAKING YOUR LETTER STAND OUT

Choosing the right paper

The actual paper you use is important. Scruffy, small format, lined paper just won't suffice for important correspondence, hence the importance of investing in some sheets of A4. The thicker the paper the better the effect, so ask your local stationer's if they have any 80 gsm quality notepaper.

If you have headed notepaper of this size by all means use it — though to include the family crest might be regarded as over the top! However, there is no need to go out of your way to get notepaper especially printed for this purpose — unless you are setting up a business. If you are applying for a job, it is far better to concentrate on layout and content.

What about colour? The conventional view is that you should stick to white, but there is no reason why you should do so. A4 paper is obtainable in a variety of tasteful colours and your letter will stand out from a sea of white paper if you decide to defy convention. Blue is to be avoided since it does not photocopy well.

Typing versus handwriting

Should your letter be typed? That depends on your handwriting. If you have a legible and neat hand, it could create a very good impression. Indeed, a few employers specify that the letter should be handwritten. A large organisation may even have a tame graphologist standing by who can assess your character from the way you dot your 'i's and cross your 't's.

On the whole it is better to type a letter — provided the result is not reminiscent of a battlefield bespattered with generous amounts of correction fluid. Thanks to the advent of word processors even amateur typists can produce very professional looking letters these days. If you do tackle the typing yourself, make certain that the layout is neat and logical.

The word processor can be a boon to the amateur typist, since you can delete words and rearrange your text in any way you like if your first attempt does not please you. You can often choose different printing styles — like *italic* or **bold** — and after careful editing you should be able to print out a letter which is immaculate and free of mistakes.

Getting the content right

We come now to the content of the letter — your 'blurb', as it were. Remember that you have to encourage the recipient to go on to the next stage — the CV or brochure (if you are setting up a business).

Try to introduce a hint of originality into your text. I am not suggesting you should list your finer points in verse, but a touch of humour in the right place or a deft turn of phrase might strike a chord with a selector or client.

If you resort to well worn formulae, hackneyed phrases and tedious sentences the selectors will merely yawn and cease to be interested.

How can you make your letter stand out? In the case of job applications the following points should be borne in mind.

- **Keep it short and to the point**. Five page epistles are out. A maximum of half a dozen concise paragraphs should more than suffice.

- **Be enthusiastic**. Start off by expressing enthusiasm for the job in order to show strong commitment. A half-hearted approach may provoke a half-hearted reaction. So start off not with the words 'with reference to. . .' but 'I should very much like to be considered. . .' or another positive phrase.

- **Explain why you want the job**. It is not because you want a good pension, help with your mortgage or a company car, but because it represents an outstanding opportunity to make full use of your considerable skills within a dynamic company. Go overboard a bit, since firms appreciate a degree of flattery.

- **Mention three or four of your outstanding features**. Be careful, though. The fact that you once played cricket or hockey for Surrey, or that you have been with the same firm for the past twenty-five years, will leave a prospective employer absolutely cold. *You* may be proud of these achievements, but are they *relevant*? No.

Do not rattle off a list of the jobs you have held. Concentrate on you **skills** and **achievements**, highlighting those that are of particular relevance to the job you are after. Use action verbs like *initiated, developed, extended, increased, established.*

If the job is in Shanghai, point to your five years' experience in Hong Kong. If the firm relies a good deal on information technology, mention how you successfully introduced a computerised system for one of your previous employers.

Avóid drawing attention to any potential weaknesses. To state you want a post overseas because your spouse has just walked out on you will suggest you are a problem candidate. Similarly, 'I admit I failed my accountancy exams, but I hope you will give me a try,' is unlikely to convince an employer that you are the ideal candidate.

- **End on a positive note**. Don't 'hope to hear from you soon', as this suggests that you are not confident that you will receive a reply. Why not 'I look forward to meeting you to discuss the contribution I can make to the continued success of your organisation.'?

If you are a businessperson in the making, you will have little need of a model letter to give you ideas for the initial contact. You will probably have received half a dozen persuasive letters yourself during the last week or so from companies seeking your custom. Instead of throwing them straight into the waste paper basket, study them carefully. Take note of the various approaches they use, and keep the ones which seem to stand out from the others. You may be able to adapt the format of some of the best when you get down to the task of contacting potential clients yourself.

COMPARING LETTERS

Your letter of application is the first step towards making a relationship with a prospective employer. If the letter fails to strike a chord that relationship will never get started.

Look at the following three letters. Which one impresses you, and why? For comments see page 179.

LETTER 1

The Dovecote,
Forest Way,
Sherwood,
Notts.

10th May 1198

The Lord Chancellor,
Westminster Palace,
Westminster,
London SW1

Dear Sir,

With reference to your advertisement in the *Sherwood Times* for a sheriff, I wish to apply for this post. Please find enclosed my CV.

Yours faithfully

Robin Hood

Fig. 3 (a). Sample application letter.

LETTER 2

Tel: Sherwood 007

The Dovecote,
Forest Way,
Sherwood,
Notts.

10th May 1198

The Lord Chancellor,
Westminster Palace,
Westminster,
London SW1A 0AA

Dear Sir,

I wish to apply for the post of Sheriff of Nottingham.

I am a graduate in law and administration of the University of
Paris and also have a diploma in forestry from the Dean
Forestry Institute.

Until two years ago I was manager of a large estate in
Nottinghamshire. Since then I have been Project Director of the
Sherwood Forest Co-operative.

Yours faithfully,

Robin Hood

Fig. 3 (b). Sample application letter.

LETTER 3

Tel: Sherwood 007

The Dovecote,
Forest Way,
Sherwood,
Notts.

The Lord Chancellor,
Westminster Palace,
Westminster,
London SW1

10th May 1198

Dear Sir,

Thank you for sending me details of the vacant post of Sheriff of Nottingham. I should like to confirm my candidature for this post as I am keen to meet new challenges and do worthwhile work in a part of the country with which I have strong associations.

As you would expect of a graduate from the University of Paris I have a sound grasp of legal matters and administrative procedures which the post clearly demands. Moreover my Diploma in Forestry has alerted me to such vital areas of concern as conservation.

You may be interested to know that I successfully managed the family estate for several years and gained plenty of 'hands on' experience. By introducing better financial controls I increased revenue by 80 per cent over a five year period.

More recently I have established a co-operative designed to combat poverty, which has already gained a considerable reputation for its innovatory techniques. In addition to the day to day management tasks, I am responsible for public relations, training and the motivation of a 50 strong task force.

I look forward to meeting you to discuss the position in greater detail.

Yours faithfully,

Robin Hood

Fig. 3 (c). Sample application letter. For the solution to this Discussion Point please turn to page 179.

WRITING SPECULATIVE LETTERS

It sometimes pays to approach employers obliquely — by expressing an interest in the firm rather than asking for a job. Such an approach will avoid embarrassment all round if there are no vacancies available, and is more likely to land you an appointment.

Although we live in the age of the telephone, your initial contact should be by letter, followed up perhaps at a later date with a phone call. Your aim must be to get your foot in the door and keep it there.

Do not be disappointed or annoyed if you are not granted an appointment. Some organisations are just too busy to be able to deal with casual visitors. On the other hand, if one expresses an interest in seeing you, you will be on the right track.

How to 'interview' a possible employer

Confirm the arrangements and think out a few pertinent questions designed to extract information on the firm and job prospects. Remember, *you* are setting out to interview *them* rather than they you.

Here are a few points you might consider:

- How do you see the business developing in the next few years?
- What skills are you going to need in the future?
- What kind of qualifications do you demand of your applicants?
- What training do you offer your staff?
- Is there any particular career pattern for employees?
- Do you have any literature about the organisation?
- What other people do you suggest that I meet?
- When and how do you recruit staff?

Avoid asking: 'Can you offer me a job?' This is like putting a pistol to your host's head. The host will immediately realise that you have an ulterior motive in setting up the visit, and this is likely to count against you. Remember, this is an exploratory interview and you should not expect to progress any further than that at this stage.

By all means mention that you are interested in applying for a job similar to the ones available in the firm, and by all means leave a copy of your CV on the desk of your host. But leave it at that — unless the person you have been talking to happens to pull a job offer out of the hat.

Tel. 0111 654321

5 Stag Walk,
Foxborough,
Moleshire MS1 2ZA

29 February 19...

R. C. Voles, Esq.,
Chief Executive,
Hareshill District Council,
Badger Parade,
Hareshill

Dear Mr Voles,

I have recently returned to the area after several years abroad working for the government of Katastrofia, and am currently looking into career opportunities in local government.

I therefore wonder if it would be possible to visit the Council offices some time in order to see how you operate and find out the kind of opportunities that might arise for a person with my qualifications and experience. I enclose my CV.

If you or one of your colleagues could spare the time to see me (with no obligation, of course), I would be most grateful. I will telephone your office next week to make an appointment.

I look forward to meeting you.

Yours sincerely,

H.G. Hogg

Fig. 4 (a). Sample speculative letter.

Tel. 0111 654321

5 Stag Walk,
Foxborough,
Moleshire MS1 2ZA

10th March 19...

R C Voles, Esq.,
Chief Executive,
Hareshill District Council,
Badger Parade,
Hareshill

Dear Mr Voles,

Thank you very much for seeing me yesterday and going into such detail as to how the District Council works. I must say I was very impressed by the smooth running of your outfit and the high degree of motivation among your staff.

I was particularly interested in the work of the planning and recreation departments. This is very much in line with the sort of responsibilities I had in Katastrofia, and I have decided to explore career possibilities in this area. I shall keep you informed of my progress.

Yours sincerely,

H.G. Hogg

Fig. 4 (b). Sample follow-up letter.

You may not have secured a post, but you should have made at least one or two contacts, and learned something about the operation of the organisation including recruitment policy and procedures. Inside knowledge of this kind will stand you in good stead should you be invited for an interview there in the future.

At all costs try to make a favourable impression on your hosts and leave the best of friends. While you should not build up your hopes too much, it is conceivable that they may write back to you in the future to enquire if you are interested in a position in the firm.

Remember to write a letter of thanks (see example). This is not only a courtesy; it also serves to keep your name to the fore.

CASE STUDIES

Angela worries about what to say

Angela feels there is little information to put in the initial application letter since her experience of the world of work is relatively limited. However a well written business-like letter, in which she shows enthusiasm for and interest in the job for which she is applying, will make a very positive impression.

Bob draws attention to his skills

Bob has already acquired certain skills relevant to the job (*eg* the ability to analyse information, to write persuasively) and he needs to draw attention to these. Employers are looking for young people with good qualifications (which Bob has) and some work experience (*eg* vacation jobs). These two items need to be mentioned in Bob's letter.

Colin brings out his achievements

By this stage in his career Colin has a number of achievements under his belt and he needs to draw attention to the most significant of these in the letter. He also needs to offer a convincing reason as to why he now wishes to move on without sounding negative about his current employers. Colin needs to show his keenness to take on greater challenges, more responsibility and the chance to broaden his experience with the firm to which he is applying.

Doreen has more skills than she realises

Doreen feels she has little to offer to the world of business, yet over the years she has reared a family successfully, managed a housekeeping budget of several thousand pounds, and organised numerous events for the local branch of the Townswomen's guild. She needs to highlight these skills and show that she is preparing for the return to the workplace by taking one or two courses.

Edward keeps it relevant

Edward has such a wealth of experience behind him that he is tempted to put it all down in his letter. In fact, he needs to prune the details drastically and only include information relevant to the job he has in mind. Reference to any courses he has taken recently will suggest to prospective employers that he takes training seriously and is reasonably up to date.

6
Your Sales Brochure

Your application letter was designed to whet the appetite. The accompanying curriculum vitae (sometimes called a CV, personal history or résumé) should provide an appetising main course, during which the recruiter checks your details to make sure you are as good as you sound. If the CV turns out to be a lengthy, poorly presented document, the recruiter could quickly have second thoughts about taking matters further.

The preparation of either document is a laborious process. Many people do not get down to compiling a CV until they start to apply for jobs, but that is rather late in the day. Now that word processors are so widespread, try to have an 'on going' CV on file which you update at regular intervals — at least once a year. In these uncertain times you never know when you are going to need it.

Presentation and content need close attention; if you already have a version of your CV on file you can tailor it to suit any job you apply for. If you only have access to a typewriter you may have to content yourself with one or two all-purpose versions of your CV which you photocopy, otherwise the exercise will be a time-consuming chore.

If you are thinking in terms of self-employment you will need to consider getting it professionally designed and printed.

WHAT TO PUT IN YOUR CV

Some people confuse the expression 'personal history' with 'autobiography', and believe you have to write reams about yourself. Not so! If you can confine your details to one side of A4 paper the selectors will bless you. Even if you are coming to the end of a rich and varied career, it should be possible to compress your achievements on to one or two pages without missing out significant details.

Main sections
What should a CV contain? The more conventional kind will be divided up into four or five sections:

- **Section 1: Personal details**, such as your name, address, telephone number, date of birth. (It is not necessary to mention marital status, ethnic group, or religious affiliation. Indeed some countries, *eg* the United States, have anti-discriminatory employment laws which forbid such information.)

- **Section 2: Education and qualifications**. Normally you need to give details of certificates and diplomas you have obtained and where you studied. Include any training you have received during the past few years.

- **Section 3: Employment history**. Here you need to give a brief description of the jobs you have held and the employer. Go into greater detail over appointments held during the past five years.

- **Section 4: Additional details**. This is a catch-all section in which you include other information which could be of relevance to the post, for example languages spoken, countries lived in or visited, pastimes indulged in, and additional skills (*eg* the ability to drive).

A further section might be included between Sections One and Two in which your skills or areas of expertise are listed. This might be particularly sensible for an older job seeker.

Listing your assets

How do you set about putting together a CV? It is vital to set aside plenty of time for the task. A CV is not the kind of document that you can produce in a matter of minutes; indeed it can involve hours of careful drafting and editing. Find a large sheet of paper and you are ready to start.

1. List in chronological order all the jobs you have ever held including part-time or temporary positions. Leave plenty of space between each item. Don't omit anything, even the painful experiences.

2. After each job write down details of the **responsibilities** you had, the **skills** you deployed and your **achievements** during each of these periods of employment. Do not forget the seemingly insignificant details, such as the time you were involved in wage negotiations or acted as your departmental representative on the sports and social club committee.

3. Try to recall all your **spare time activities**. If you were once the lead trombonist in your college jazz band, note it down. The same applies if you have been events organiser of your local skittles club, chairman of the local Residents' Association, a district councillor, a churchwarden, or anything of this nature; the skills you used in your various capacities could well be relevant to some of the jobs you are after.

4. List your **educational achievements** — not only the diplomas and certificates which are gathering dust in your bottom drawer, but also the different courses you have attended more recently — whether this was training in management, first aid or civil defence.

By now you should have assembled an impressive amount of information about yourself. If you haven't, enlist the help of a trusted colleague and have a brain-storming session. If you cannot give a good account of yourself, there may be others who can.

Sorting out the details

Your next task is going to prove even harder. Take a hard look at all the information you have put down on the sheet of paper and try to categorise them. You might well decide on four categories, such as

- very significant
- fairly significant
- potentially significant
- unimportant

If you have coloured pens or pencils, underline the **very significant** items in red. These are details which you feel justified in including on any CV, since they demonstrate your major skills and shed light on your character and general abilities. Interpersonal skills, specialist knowledge, management prowess deserve mention whatever position you are angling for.

The **fairly significant** items are those which you feel could prove useful but not in every eventuality. Your experience with the Territorials might be useful if you are going to work in a closely knit organisation. Your involvement with the local Scouts or Guides would be a definite plus if you are after a job that brings you in contact with young people; less so if you are trying to land a job in the City. Underline these items in green.

The **potentially significant** items are those which you would not normally include on your CV, but which could sway the balance in your favour in certain situations. If you are applying to work with an organisation with a cosmopolitan workforce, your work for the local branch of the United Nations Association might deserve a mention in your letter. Underline these in brown.

The 'unimportant' items are those aspects of your life which do not really deserve a mention in your correspondence. Do not jettison them completely, however. Some of them could be mentioned in passing at interview should a suitable occasion arise. If, for instance, the subject of sport is touched on at the interview, this might be the place for you to mention that you played rugby or netball for your college.

PREPARING THE DOCUMENT EFFECTIVELY

Drafting the CV

Now that you have assembled all the data, start transferring it to a clean sheet of paper using the headings suggested on page 58 of this chapter. If you have a word processor at your disposal key it straight onto the disk, otherwise continue to work in longhand. Aim to contain the information on a single sheet of A4 paper.

You may find that the information overruns the page, in which case you will need to do some pruning. Try to summarise your activities that belong to the dim and distant past and put emphasis on what you have done over the past five or ten years. When you have finished, ask a friend to pass a critical eye over it and let you know whether he feels it does you justice.

For instance, are your responsibilities and achievements clearly shown? A simple job title is meaningless. the titles 'manager', 'secretary', 'engineer', 'supervisor' can cover a multitude of sins or hide a considerable record of achievement. For the more recent jobs, at least, you need to describe your responsibilities and mention your achievements.

Pepper your prose with strong verbs such as *activate, contribute, establish, extend, improve, implement, initiate, increase, lead, negotiate, overhaul, restructure.* They will help to show that you have made an active contribution to the success of the organisations for which you have worked. A few adjectives such as *challenging, innovative, successful* would also help to promote a positive image of yourself.

Check the details carefully to ensure there isn't a hint of failure in the whole document. Does the CV give the impression of a steady

PERSONAL HISTORY: SAMANTHA MORRIS

HOME ADDRESS: The Lilacs, Acacia Avenue, Abbots Oak, Willowshire
            WW3 7WW
            (Telephone: 0999 54321)

ADDRESS FOR CORRESPONDENCE (until July): Hollyhock Hall,
            Delphinium College, Tulipville, Astershire AA9 BB2
            (Telephone: 0111 22222 ext 33)

DATE OF BIRTH: 31 December 1968

EDUCATION
1983 - 1988   Larch Rise School, Abbots Oak
1988 - 1990   Abbots Oak Sixth Form College
1990 -   Delphinium University College, Tulipville

QUALIFICATIONS
1988   GCSE: History (A), English Language (B), Biology (B),
                   Geography (C), Mathematics (C), Chemistry (C),
                   Chinese (C).
1990   GCE 'A' Level: Biology (B), Chemistry (C), Geography (C)

I am currently studying for BSc in Botany, and will take my Finals later this
year.

WORK EXPERIENCE
1989 & 1990   Shop Assistant at Peony Fabrics, Abbots Oak.
                   This was a vacation job which lasted for five weeks.
1991   Deputy Manager, Petunia Garden Centre, Abbots Oak
                   Another vacation job of two months' duration. I was pro-
                   moted to the position of Deputy Manager after four weeks.
1992   Tourist Guide, Daffodil Tours Ltd
                   A three month vacation job in which I accompanied coach
                   tours of foreign tourists on visits to leading gardens
                   throughout the country.

INTERESTS
Hockey: I have recently been appointed captain of the college Hockey XI
Judo: I am secretary of the Delphinium College Judo Club
Writing: I am a reporter on the college newspaper.

OTHER INFORMATION
I possess a clean driving licence, speak Chinese and Hungarian, and have
travelled to India, Spain and Morocco. I shall be free to take up an appointment from July onwards.

Fig. 5 (a). Model CV 1.

Curriculum Vitae of ROBIN HOOD

ADDRESS: The Dovecote, Forest Way, Sherwood, Notts.
TEL: Sherwood Forest 0007
DATE OF BIRTH: 30th November 1170

EDUCATION AND QUALIFICATIONS

1181-87	Nottingham High School	School Certificate in French, English, Latin, Maths, Music, Philosophy.
1187-90	University of Paris	Bachelor of Law (with distinction).
1190-91	University of Genoa	Diploma in Forestry

EXPERIENCE AND ACHIEVEMENTS

1191-96   Fitzwarren Estate: Manager.
My duties included overseeing the work of 30 men, budgeting, financial planning, and sales management.
During the period I introduced new flexi-time work rotas; increased crop yields by 30 per cent; designed and implemented a new management control system; and successfully integrated part of a neighbouring estate into the business.

1196-   The Lincoln Green Co-operative: Founder and Chief Executive
This is a relatively new organisation which I set up with a view to relieving poverty and hardship in the Sherwood Forest area.
I have been responsible for recruitment; training and supervision of fifty social workers and ancillary staff; public relations; financial management.
The organisation has already made a substantial contribution to the redistribution of wealth in the county.

FURTHER INFORMATION

Hobbies:	Fencing, riding and archery. (I have won three cups in archery contests during the last four years.)
Countries visited:	France, Switzerland and Italy.
Languages:	French (fluent); Italian (fairly good).
Health:	Extremely robust. I have experienced no serious illnesses.

I am able to attend for interview at any time given a week's notice.

Fig. 5 (b). Model CV 2.

Offer for Sale

MAKE/MODEL:	ADRIAN ST JOHN CARRUTHERS
YEAR:	September 1935
LOCATION:	15 Brooklands Terrace, Austin Parva, Humberside.
CONDITION:	First class after a recent overhaul.
DIMENSIONS:	6ft 1in.

SPECIFICATIONS:
1953   School Certificate (Eton)
1955   C & G Engineering Diploma (Dingwall Technical College)
1964   MBA (Manchester Business School)

MAIN FEATURES:
Experienced negotiator; all-round ability; knowledge of international motor trade; fluent in Greek and Japanese

PREVIOUS OWNERS:
1953-56	Rolls Royce, Crewe: Engineering Apprentice
1956-58	Ford, Dagenham: Fitter
1958-62	General Motors, Detroit, USA: Assembly Supervisor
1964-70	Le Mans Auto Sales, Dublin: General Manager
1970-75	Racetrack Engineering, Holyhead: Marketing Manager
1983-present	Toyota International, Tokyo: Deputy Export Manager

NOTE:
From 1976 to 1982 I ran my own firm, Carruthers Car Components (Cobham) Ltd, which I later sold.

EXTRAS:
Winner of 'Salesman of the Year Award' 1969
Member of the British Institute of Management

VALUE:
Approximately £35,000 per annum. Best offer secures. Telephone: 0123 12121 (24 hour answering service).

Fig. 5 (c). Alternative model CV.

63

Profile of

DAVID ROBERT PHILLIPS

David Phillips was born in Swansea in 1953 and attended Fishguard High School where he was successful at six subjects at GCE Ordinary Level. He then studied at Cardiff Technical College for a Higher National Diploma (a post high school qualification) in Telecommunications. Four years later he obtained a City & Guilds certificate in Supervisory Management.

After qualifying in telecommunications he worked for the Post Office (now British Telecom) as a telecommunications engineer for ten years before moving to Tanzania where he was a telecommunications instructor at Dar es Salaam Polytechnic for three years under contract to the Overseas Development Administration (the British Government's aid agency).

On returning to England he joined Ogden Electronics in Bedford as Overseas Sales Manager with particular responsibility for Africa and Southern Europe. He negotiated a number of important contracts for the provision and installation of telecommunications equipment with the governments of Burundi, Chad, Lesotho and Andorra.

Ogden Electronics was taken over by its main rival last year and this resulted in large scale redundancies among company employees, including David Phillips. Since parting company with the firm he has taken a distance learning course in satellite communication techniques with the Open College and obtained a certificate in management from the Institute of Management.

David Phillips is a person with wide interests. He plays the trombone in the local Salvation Army Band, and is honorary treasurer of a local working men's club. He is a member of Bedford Rotary Club and is well known in the area for his fundraising efforts for local charities.

He is now looking for a contract with a progressive firm that is able to make full use of his qualifications and experience in the field of telecommunications or management.

Fig. 5 (d). Career Profile.

career progression? — which is what employers by and large like to see. If not, you may need to do some further work on the document.

A good CV not only has to read well; it has to look good. It needs to be typed (or word-processed) and clearly set out. Most people use white paper, but there is no reason why you should not use light coloured paper. Perk the design up, if you wish, particularly if you are applying for a job where flamboyance or artistic flair are called for. Some selectors appreciate CVs which are a little out of the ordinary, provided the flair does not obscure the details.

Choosing the right format
Have a look at the CVs on pages 61 to 64. Which one would you choose for your CV? How might each of the documents be improved? For comments see the Appendix, page 180.

CASE STUDIES

Angela finds things to include
Angela may feel there is very little she can put on her CV apart from her GCSE results. However, she has some work experience: she has a Saturday job as a sales assistant and worked full-time in the local library for three weeks last summer. Both jobs deserve a mention in Section 3 of the CV. In Section 4 she should include her school activities and responsibilities (she is a prefect and captain of the school hockey team) and mention her charity work (she raises funds for the local branch of the Save the Children Fund (see Model CV 1).

Bob worries about his work experience
Section 2 of Bob's CV is more impressive than Angela's and much longer, but the work experience section looks rather thin. However he has done one or two interesting vacation jobs which show that he is good at handling people. For instance, last summer he was a camp leader at a children's summer camp in the United States and the previous year he worked as a night porter in a London hotel. While this may not qualify him to manage the London Hilton, it does suggest that he is both responsible and resourceful (see Model CV 1).

Colin focuses on his strengths
The longest part of Colin's CV should be Section 3, where he should describe his work, his responsibilities and achievements in some depth. In the qualifications section he should include any courses that he has attended recently, either in-house training or evening classes.

He should beware of putting down too many interests, as this could suggest to a prospective employer that his work takes second place to his hobbies (see Model CV 2).

Doreen shows what she can do

Doreen is afraid there is a yawning gap in the middle of Section 3. Yet for the past 15 years she has been a housewife and mother, an occupation as full-time as any other. It involved a wide and demanding range of skills such as budgeting, counselling, catering, delegating, leadership, time management among many others. Why not mention it? She has also done a few courses in her spare time, and these need to be included in Section 2. Her many outside interests should be mentioned in Section 4 (*eg* treasurer of her branch of the Townswomen's Guild, voluntary worker at an old people's day centre, school governor).

Edward concentrates on the recent past

Edward should resist the temptation of spreading his CV over three pages. The early part of his career could be in summary form, and he should concentrate on what he has done over the past decade. It might be sensible to list jobs in reverse chronological order or place Section 3 before Section 2. It is hardly necessary for him to mention all the schools he attended and all the exams he passed, but any recent training should be included. Since Edward is considering the self-employment option, he might also draw up a profile of himself to circulate to potential clients. He might also try a less traditional type of CV in order to attract attention, (see Model CV 2, Alternative CV and Profile).

7
Dealing with Application Forms

UNDERSTANDING APPLICATION FORMS

Having written an impeccable letter of application and constructed a workmanlike CV, you could be forgiven for believing that your efforts to date should suffice for the company or organisation on which you are keen to bestow your talents.

Yet you have reckoned without that printed document which is the scourge of all job-seekers — the application form. On this you are expected to reproduce all the details that appear on your CV — and more.

There is, alas, no such thing as a standard application form. If there were, life would be so much simpler. Some forms are designed quite well with enough space to enter all the relevant points relating to your career. But others resemble an ill-fitting suit with not enough space to cram in your answers to important questions but plenty of room set aside for matters which do not apply to you.

Application forms have a purpose
The big temptation is either to tear the form up or write across it: 'Please refer to CV'. This is a sure way of engaging the wrath of the selectors, one of whom probably drew up the wretched document and regards it as the crowning achievement of a lifetime. No, you will have to knuckle under and fill it in.

Believe it or not, such forms do serve a useful purpose. For instance, it is much easier for the selection board to compare the attributes and experience of competing candidates if their details are set down in a standard format.

For the applicant, too, there are benefits. Application forms tend to concentrate the mind on providing the information which the firm appears to need rather than the details you think they ought to have. This may stimulate you to recall aspects of your experience that you have forgotten to include in your CV.

Reading the form through

Completing an application form is not a matter to be hurried over. If you try to complete it in five minutes, you will only make mistakes and have to make corrections. For instance, you might insert your telephone number in the box marked 'date of birth' or detail the salaries you have received in the column 'reason for leaving'. Don't make a mess. Treat the form with respect.

If you are a methodical person, you may decide to make a photocopy of the document first of all and complete this as well as you can before tackling the original. If you are disinclined to go to these lengths, at least read through the form, making notes as you do so, before committing pen to paper.

The first part of the form will require the sort of data which is already on your CV, so make certain you have this beside you.

Some forms have a second part which asks questions designed to learn more about your character or health — questions such as:

- What attracts you to this post?
- What do you hope to achieve if offered the post?
- What experience of yours is particularly relevant to the job?
- What is your long-term ambition?
- What serious illnesses have you suffered in the past five years?

Finally, you may have to sign a statement saying that you have completed the form truthfully and to the best of your ability. If you have deliberately put down misleading information, your application could be disqualified.

Choosing your references

On most forms you are expected to include the names of two or three referees — people who can either confirm the details on the form or comment on your character or your suitability for the post.

There is some dispute in personnel circles as to how reliable character references really are. After all, a candidate is hardly going to cite a referee who will give him a bad reference.

For this reason some organisations rely very little on references. On the other hand, some selectors pay considerable heed to the opinions of referees. Since you cannot know in advance what line the selectors are going to take you should choose your referees with care.

Who should you approach for a reference? They will normally fit in one of the following categories.

- Someone who can comment on your education (*ie* an academic referee). This is particularly important if you are following a course or have completed one during the past few years.

- Someone who can comment on your work, such as your immediate superior or employer. Otherwise it could be someone with whom you have had dealings on a professional basis.

- Someone who knows you well outside the workplace, such as your local councillor, parish priest or the chairman of an association to which you belong. The social standing of the person matters less than his ability to communicate effectively about you.

Your referees, whoever they are, are doing you a favour by offering to write a reference. Make sure first that they are willing to help out in this way, and keep them informed of your progress. If you supply them with an up-to-date CV and details of the post for which you are applying, they will be able to tailor their reference accordingly.

Do not confuse a reference with an **open testimonial**. Generally speaking, such communications carry little weight with selectors simply because they lack confidentiality. The exception is where you are self-employed and need to show that your work is satisfactory to prospective clients.

COMPLETING THE FORM

Once you have finished the preliminaries, you must decide how to set out the information on the form. This may appear straightforward, but don't bank on it. It is pointless going into a lengthy description of your past responsibilities if there are only three inches of space available. You either have to prune the details drastically or enter them on a separate sheet.

Read the instructions
First read the instructions at the top carefully. If black ink or black typescript are specified, it makes sense to comply, otherwise your details may not be reproduced too well if the form is photocopied. By all means type the information, if you are a skilled practitioner able to align the typewriter or word-processor correctly. If you are not, this

APPLICATION FORM

POST APPLIED FOR: _REF M439_

NAME   (SURNAME) ROBINSON (FIRST NAMES) JACK

ADDRESS (PERMANENT) 8 PINE CLOSE (FOR CORRESPONDENCE) _____

SEVENOAKS SV3 5ZZ

TELEPHONE NUMBER 0999 543210

SEX _____ M

NATIONALITY _BRITISH_

DATE OF BIRTH _29.2.71_

PLACE OF BIRTH _WHITCHURCH_

MARITAL STATUS _ENGAGED_

EDUCATION

DATES	INSTITUTION	QUALIFICATIONS ACHIEVED
1976-78	GREENFIELD PRIMARY SCHOOL SEVENOAKS	
1978-82	BLACKSTONE PRIMARY SCHOOL LUTON	SWIMMING CERT. GOOD CONDUCT CERT.
1982-89	REDHILL HIGH SCHOOL DONCASTER	GCSE : LATIN, ENGLISH, FRENCH, MATHS, BIOLOGY, SOCIAL STUDIES. A-LEVEL : ECONOMICS, HISTORY, MA
1989-92	UNIVERSITY OF IPSWICH	BA HONS (CRYPTOLOGY)

EMPLOYMENT HISTORY

DATES	EMPLOYER'S NAME & ADDRESS	TITLE & RESPONSIBILITIES	REASON FOR LEAVING
1992-	GRABBIT & CO SILVER STREET LONDON EC3 4SZ	ASSISTANT STOCKBROKER	I HAVEN'T LEFT YET!

Fig. 6. Sample application form (completed).

MEMBERSHIP OF PROFESSIONAL ASSOCIATIONS ___*N. A.*___

ADDITIONAL TRAINING COURSES ATTENDED *FIRST AID COURSE, ST. JOHN'S AMBULANCE*

HOBBIES, SPORTS & OTHER INTERESTS *SQUASH, TENNIS, BADMINTON, POLITICS, THEATRE, MUSIC*

DO YOU HOLD A CURRENT DRIVING LICENCE?   *YES.*

HAVE YOU SUFFERED ANY SERIOUS ILLNESSES DURING THE PAST FIVE YEARS? IF SO GIVE DETAILS.

SPRAINED ANKLE   1990
INFLUENZA   1992

DO YOU HAVE ANY CONVICTIONS OTHER THAN FOR MINOR OFFENCES? IF SO GIVE DETAILS.

PARKING FINE   1993   CHESTER

SUPPLY THE NAMES AND ADDRESSES OF THREE PEOPLE WHO CAN COMMENT ON YOUR SUITABILITY FOR THE POST

A. XERXES	*J. YOUNG*	*R. ZEPHANIAH*
10 GRECIAN WAY	*STORNAWAY COLLEGE*	*12 ROMAN ST.*
DUNSTABLE DB3 4NS	*ISLE OF SKYE*	*DONCASTER DC3 4AA*

EXPLAIN BRIEFLY WHY YOU WISH TO BE CONSIDERED FOR THIS POST AND WHAT EXPERTISE YOU COULD BRING TO IT

I DO NOT LIKE MY CURRENT JOB VERY MUCH, AND NEED A CHANGE. THE POST YOU ARE OFFERING SOUNDS ATTRACTIVE AND WOULD ALLOW ME TO MAKE BETTER USE OF MY SKILLS.

I AFFIRM THAT TO THE BEST OF MY KNOWLEDGE THE INFORMATION GIVEN ABOVE IS CORRECT.

SIGNED ___*J Robinson*___ DATE ___*31. 4. 94*___

can be a fiddly business and you may do better by writing in the details clearly and neatly.

Certain sections need to be completed in block letters, so make sure you glance against each section in turn before you get to work on it. Try to answer all the questions; if any do not apply to you enter 'Not applicable' or 'N/A'. If precise dates (day, month and year) are required, you must enter them.

Be relevant

Avoid exaggerated claims, and do not list all your leisure-time pursuits if they are very numerous. Certainly leave out things which might raise an eyebrow, such as fire-eating or membership of a witches' coven! Make sure that every statement you make is basically true, since false declarations could result in your application being disqualified.

There is no obligation to fill every square inch of the paper. You do not, for example, have to include every illness you have ever suffered in the medical section, unless you wish to be regarded as a hypochondriac. Only serious illnesses which have involved a prolonged period of convalescence deserve a mention. Nor need you dwell on the reasons for leaving your former position.

At the end of this time-consuming chore, read through the form again carefully, checking for such things as spelling errors. If you feel it is a true and balanced account of yourself, sign and date it. However, if you feel that you have had to omit significant items about yourself owing to lack of space, you could attach an extra sheet of paper with this information on it.

Checking the form

On pages 70-71 there is an application form which has been completed. Has the applicant done a good job or not? Compare your comments with those in the Appendix, page 180.

Despatching your application

You should now have your documents ready to put in an envelope for despatch: your letter of application, your CV and your completed application form. Give them a final going-over, and when you are satisfied, fold them neatly and put them in a decent-sized envelope.

Make sure that you have addressed the envelope and its contents to the right person at the right address, stick a first class stamp on it and head for the nearest post box. If you are anxious lest your efforts get lost in the post you could send them recorded delivery.

APPLICATION FORM

POST APPLIED FOR: _____

NAME   (SURNAME)_____ (FIRST NAMES) _____

ADDRESS (PERMANENT) _____ (FOR CORRESPONDENCE) _____

_____   _____

TELEPHONE NUMBER _____   _____

SEX _____

NATIONALITY _____

DATE OF BIRTH_____

PLACE OF BIRTH_____

MARITAL STATUS_____

EDUCATION

DATES	INSTITUTION	QUALIFICATIONS ACHIEVED

EMPLOYMENT HISTORY

DATES	EMPLOYER'S NAME & ADDRESS	TITLE & RESPONSIBILITIES	REASON FOR LEAVING

Fig. 7. Sample application form (blank).

MEMBERSHIP OF PROFESSIONAL ASSOCIATIONS _____

ADDITIONAL TRAINING COURSES ATTENDED _____

HOBBIES, SPORTS & OTHER INTERESTS _____

DO YOU HOLD A CURRENT DRIVING LICENCE?

HAVE YOU SUFFERED ANY SERIOUS ILLNESSES DURING THE PAST
FIVE YEARS? IF SO GIVE DETAILS.

DO YOU HAVE ANY CONVICTIONS OTHER THAN FOR MINOR OF-
FENCES? IF SO GIVE DETAILS.

SUPPLY THE NAMES AND ADDRESSES OF THREE PEOPLE WHO
CAN COMMENT ON YOUR SUITABILITY FOR THE POST

_____   _____   _____

_____   _____   _____

_____   _____   _____

EXPLAIN BRIEFLY WHY YOU WISH TO BE CONSIDERED FOR THIS
POST AND WHAT EXPERTISE YOU COULD BRING TO IT

I AFFIRM THAT TO THE BEST OF MY KNOWLEDGE THE INFORMA-
TION GIVEN ABOVE IS CORRECT.

SIGNED_____ DATE _____

You may be tempted to pat yourself on the back and go out for a celebration. By all means do so, since you will have expended a fair amount of time and effort. But first file away all your handiwork together with the job description. You may need to refer to this information again before long.

Do not expect to wait for a favourable reply inviting you for an interview with all expenses paid. The odds are that you will just receive a polite note thanking you for your interest and regretting that you are not on the shortlist. Unfortunately many people will be in the same situation.

But you have been forewarned about this problem. You will have to repeat the application process time and again. Application forms are going to become a familiar phenomenon!

Application form practice

On pages 73-74 there is an application form (fig. 7.) for you to photocopy and practise filling in. Consider what impression it is likely to make on a recipient and try to identify ways in which the information could be improved.

CASE STUDIES

Angela: referees for school leavers

Whether she applies for a job, or a course at a university or college, Angela will need to include referees on her application form. One of them will be her school principal or house-master/mistress. If another referee is needed, it ideally needs to be a person of some standing who knows her well — the local vicar, the branch chairman of the SCF for which she has done fund rasing, or the manager of the shop where she works on Saturdays. Her Uncle Vernon, who is a JP, might sound ideal, but she cannot use relatives for this purpose.

Bob needs more than academic referees

Bob has a batch of people to choose from, mainly with an academic background. He will need to cite his tutor or head of department at university; it would look suspicious if he did not mention one or the other. But there may be other people who know him as well: the college chaplain, for instance, of the manager of the children's holiday camp he worked at.

Colin's need for confidentiality

Colin is in a quandary. By rights he should include his current employer in his list of referees, but is reluctant at this stage to reveal that he is looking for another job. Some firms overcome this difficulty by promising on the form not to approach referees without prior permission, but many do not. If not, Colin should make it clear either on the form or in a covering note that his employer should not be approached — for the time being at least. Fortunately he has built up a number of contacts in business or society at large who would be prepared to recommend him.

Doreen scratches around for ideas

Doreen wonders who on earth she can cite as a referee. The people who know her best — her family — are excluded on the grounds of relationship. She cannot use the name of her old headmistress, since she is dead; but in any case her school days finished long ago and she needs people who have known her more recently. How about the tutor on her evening course, the supervisor of the day centre she helps at, the local parish priest, or the chairman of the local Townswomen's Guild?

Edward considers his options

Edward, like Colin, does not want to include his current employer among his referees, though there is a manager in another department who is a close friend and may be a passable substitute. He also has a number of useful contacts outside the firm — in the local Rotary Club, in his professional association — who would be prepared to do the honours. One or two senior staff no longer with the firm might also be worth consideration.

8
Selling Yourself
at an Interview

One of these days all your hard work so far will bear fruit, and you will be invited for an interview. This should be a cause for celebration: it means your written presentation has been effective and the organisation is impressed enough to want to see you in person.

Interview invitations can turn up when you least expect them and from a source that you may have written off long ago. Some come in letter form, but many are arranged over the telephone and are not confirmed in writing. So make sure you keep a diary handy by the telephone to check that you are free at the time suggested. You should note:

- where exactly the interview is to be held (if you do not know the area request a map)

- when the interview will start (time and date)

- whom you should ask for when you arrive

- what form the selection process is likely to take, eg panel interview, tests, group exercises (the latter two are common in civil service and military selection boards).

To avoid mistakes it is sensible to confirm that you will be attending at the time and place attended in writing.

PREPARING YOURSELF FOR AN INTERVIEW

Finding out about the organisation
Having surmounted the first hurdle you need to look ahead to the second fence which will prove much trickier. You may not have paid much attention to the organisation that wants to see you so far, but now you need to research it thoroughly so as to be well informed at the interview.

You will get some idea of the organisation from the literature that they produce about themselves — annual reports and such like. With any luck you will have received a job description together with some background material on the organisation, but if you haven't do not hesitate to contact the personnel or public relations department to see if this information is available.

If you have little or no information and time is pressing, make a bee-line for your local reference library to research the organisation, enlisting the aid of the librarian, if necessary. The librarian will be able to point you in the direction of books like the *Kompass Register of British Industry and Commerce*, Dun and Bradstreet's *Guide to Key British Enterprises* and *The Times Top 1000 Companies*. *The Good Job Guide* and Extel cards are other good sources of information.

One keen job-hunter trekked down to Companies' House in London for the most recent report of the firm with which he was to have an interview.

Nowadays, you could save yourself time by finding a local library that has on-line access to that organisation's database. For the most up-to-date knowledge, scrutinise recent issues of professional journals related to the firm's line of expertise and yours.

If you can track down any employees (or former employees) of the company who are willing to give you some inside knowledge, by all means consult them. People will often talk quite openly about their jobs and employers, though some comments have to be taken with a pinch of salt.

Do not confine yourself to the company itself. It could be well worth your while to discover what competitors are up to and what their current standing is in their particular sector. As an outsider you may turn up some facts that your interviewers are not aware of, which will mark you out at the interview as someone knowledgeable and interested in the firm.

Assessing the organisation

While the main motive behind your research is to help you shine at your interview, try to assess what the organisation can offer you. Here are some of the questions you will need to find answers to:

- Does it offer the kind of environment in which I could make good use of my talents, or would I find it frustrating?

- Does the job offer security and prospects — or would it be merely a turning into a dead end?

- Does the company have an exciting future— or is it heading for the rocks?

- Is it a dynamic go-ahead organisation, or staid and conventional?

- Has it a reputation for looking after its staff and clients well — or not?

Your visit to the company will offer you a chance to confirm or refute these initial impressions.

Training in interview techniques

A title fight can be won or lost in a matter of minutes, so each contender undergoes arduous training to ensure that he is at his best on the night. Interviews are not dissimilar, and some training can help you to make a favourable impression on the selectors.

Some politicians engage professional consultants to coach them in interview techniques, and some career counselling firms can offer this facility to their clients. Careers offices, local colleges, and local job centres should be able to tell you what facilities are available. But you may also have friends or colleagues who can put you through your paces.

If you can videotape yourself you will have an opportunity to judge how you appear to others, and this can be a moment of truth. Far from being the articulate, decisive person you consider yourself to be, you may come over as a bumbling bundle of nerves with irritating mannerisms. It is up to you to try and iron out these problems before the spotlight falls on you in earnest.

Try to visualise the worst possible interview scenario where you are asked a bevy of questions which seem designed to trip you up or expose the skeletons in your cupboard. Instead of hoping that such questions do not turn up, you would be better advised to spend your time thinking of a few convincing answers — answers which will show you in a good light. You left your last job, for example, not because of a row with the boss but because of your unease regarding the firm's long-term strategy.

Questions you may be asked

Not all the following questions are designed to trip you up. Nevertheless you should make sure that you can answer them competently. How would you tackle them?

Why do you want this job?
Where do you see yourself in five years' time?
Why should we offer you the job?
What are your strengths/weaknesses?
What do you consider your greatest achievement?
Why did you leave X? *or* Why do you want to leave X?
What changes would you institute if you were offered the job?
What do you know about us?
What is your opinion of the unions, British management, etc?
What salary are you hoping for?
What sort of qualities are needed in this job?
Which aspects of the job do you feel least competent to tackle?
What additional training will you need to do the job?
Why did you choose this particular career?
What do you enjoy doing most at work/in your leisure time?
What attracts you to this firm?
What do you hope to achieve if you are appointed?
What type of management style do you favour?
Which other firms have you applied to?
What are your main leisure time pursuits?

Turn to page 181 for suggested answers and comments.
One word of warning: do not try to memorise answers to possible questions parrot fashion. An interruption or a supplementary question could throw you off course. You must be prepared for all eventualities.

Looking good
Visual impressions count and all candidates should consider what sort of a figure they will cut in the interview room.

You will not be expected to arrive dressed up to the nines in a morning suit or the latest Dior creation, but you should try to look reasonably smart.

The secret is to dress appropriately. If you are after a farm manager's job tweeds should be quite acceptable; for an executive position you would need a dark suit or outfit; for an academic or media post more casual attire might be in order provided you do not look a scarecrow. If you are not quite sure what to wear, play safe and wear something sober.

You might also consider whether a visit to the hairdresser is not overdue, since a well groomed head of hair could make a favourable impression on your interviewers.

Finally, before you set off for the interview have a bath or a shower. Not only do you need to look good, you have to smell good, too!

Getting to the interview on time

According to the Institute of Personnel & Development one in every five job applicants arrives late for the interview; a surprising one in ten does not show up at all. Do they forget or lose their way? Heaven knows! You should leave no stone unturned to ensure that you turn up for your interview in good time and in good shape.

Leave plenty of margin for error. Trains sometimes arrive late and cars sometimes break down or become enmeshed in traffic jams. If you live in south west England and the interview is in north east Scotland, you will need to consider overnight accommodation, unless you opt to fly or there is an overnight sleeper. Driving overnight is not an option; you would need matchsticks to keep your bloodshot eyes open at the interview.

Expenses

Some employers are prepared to pay for interview expenses (*eg* travel and accommodation) but you cannot count on it. For this reason you should take advantage of cheap train fares, though you should never opt for cheapness at the expense of reliability. If you are unemployed you may be able to get your fare paid by the local Job Centre but you need to stake your claim well in advance.

Before you leave home, make sure you have:

● directions to the interview venue

● any documentation which has been requested or might be needed (*eg* a CV or samples of your work)

● a contact telephone number — just in case of emergencies.

Before the interview

It is sensible to arrive 10 or 15 minutes before the interview is due to begin, so that you have time to spruce yourself up in the wash room and relax before the ordeal.

Try to make a good impression on the secretary or the receptionist, just in case she is an *eminence grise* who assists with the decision-making. Even if she is not, this is good practice for later. Moreover she may be able to fill you in on some of the details of the interview, such as how long it is likely to take.

See if you can find out who will be interviewing you, whether you will have one interview or several, and what form the proceedings will take. Practices vary from organisation to organisation and you should be prepared to face any of the following:

Individual interviews
You are interviewed by just one person. This is less demanding than the other types of interview provided you can establish some rapport with the interviewer.

Sequential interviews
You are interviewed by a number of people in turn. This can take up a lot of time and you need to be able to adjust quickly to different personalities and techniques.

Two interviewer interviews
You are interviewed by two people together. Interviews like this can be very demanding since you have to cope with two people at the same time.

Panel interviews
You are interviewed by a panel of three or more interviewers. This can be very offputting to those of a shy or nervous disposition. You may feel like an actor appearing in front of an audience attempting to satisfy a range of tastes.

Panel interviews are very common in the public sector, but you could also face a combination of interview types, *eg* an individual interview followed by a panel interview.

ATTENDING THE INTERVIEW

Starting off the interview
It is often felt that the first two minutes of an interview are decisive, and that interviewers spend the rest of the time confirming or refuting their first impression of you. Whether this is true or not, the way you enter the room, the way you greet your interviewer(s), and your general appearance can set the tone of the interview. A muddled entry, a flabby handshake and shabby clothes could instantly condemn you to the reject file.

If the interviewer or chairman of the interview panel is an experienced practitioner, he will try to put you at ease before getting down to the nitty gritty. If you are asked whether you had a pleasant journey, this is not the moment to launch into a diatribe on the shortcomings of the public transport system. Instead, offer a conventional response.

The aim of interviewer and interviewee must be to develop mutual rapport in these initial stages. This does not mean, however, that the interview will be a cosy chat between friends, even if you do spot an acquaintance on the interviewing panel. It is essentially a business meeting and you must remain business-like throughout.

To round off the first stage of the interview the interviewer may well set the scene. This might involve giving some background on the company and outlining the responsibilities of the job for which you have applied. Once this has been completed the spotlight falls on you.

Giving a good account of yourself

Some interviewers like to take you through your CV in order to clarify matters which are not self-apparent. Be prepared for questions on the courses you have taken (if you are a young applicant) or the responsibilities you have had (if you are a mature candidate) and how they might have prepared you for the position for which you have applied.

Many will be keen to find out about you as a person — how you react to this and what you think of that. They will explore your motives for applying for the job and your ambitions for the future. Your pastimes, home life, attitudes and health could all come under scrutiny — as well as your knowledge of current affairs.

Your problem solving abilities may also be tested. You may be confronted with a hypothetical situation and asked to explain how you would deal with it (eg how to deal with a customer who is slow at paying his bills). Or you might have to refer to problems that you have faced in the past and how you managed to solve them.

If you have prepared yourself properly for the session you should be able to deal adequately with most of the questions that come your way. There will, however, be a few unexpected ones designed perhaps to test your knowledge of current affairs or your personal attitudes. If you are momentarily stumped for an answer or you can't grasp the tenor of the question, play for time by asking for it to be repeated or rephrased.

Whatever happens, keep your cool. If you can't answer the query, don't tie yourself up in knots trying to do so; this will gain you no credit at all. It is better to confess ignorance right from the start rather than try to bluff your way unconvincingly out of the situation.

Be courteous at all times; never argue; and try to keep your answers to the point, bringing in examples of your experience and achievements wherever you can.

● The secret is to sell yourself at every opportunity, without being too blatant. If you can lead the conversation in a direction which will let you elaborate on your strengths, you should seize the initiative.

Beware, however, of becoming over-confident. Some two-person interviews use a 'sweet and sour' strategy. One member of the team asks easy sympathetic questions and the other bowls the tricky ones. In panel interviews, too, there may well be someone who interrupts you in full flight with a penetrating question which brings you down to earth with a bump.

Some interviewers will be only too happy to give you your head, but not necessarily to avoid thinking of dozens of questions. An invitation to 'tell me something about yourself' is not the easy option it seems, since you can never be quite sure what the interviewer really wants to know. You are being given, in effect, enough rope to hang yourself, and a wordy complicated answer will count heavily against you.

Rounding off the interview

As the interview draws to a close you may be invited to confirm your continued interest in the job and ask questions. It is wise to bear in mind that you are still under scrutiny, and your questions should be designed to show your interest in the firm's achievements rather than the pay and conditions offered.

Even if most points have been explained thoroughly, you should still have one or two questions up your sleeve, so that the interview does not come to an abrupt end. These could be questions designed less to extract information and more to show you in a more favourable light. You could, for example, ask if there will be an opportunity for you to make use of the export marketing skills you picked up on a recent course.

Other questions you might pose include:

● To whom would I be directly responsible?
● What opportunities are there for training/career development?

- Where would the appointee be based?
- What prospects are there for promotion?
- When do you hope to make the appointment?
- What sort of response did you have to this job advertisement?

This is not the time to find out if the company is good enough for you in terms of salary, perks and working conditions, so beware of asking too many lengthy and involved questions, particularly if the interviewers seem pressed for time.

At the close of the interview you may not be informed of the result, but you should certainly be told what happens next. There should be some indication of when a decision is to be taken on your candidature and whether more interviews or tests are likely.

If first impressions matter, so do the final ones. Do make certain that the interview finishes on a high note, even if you feel parts of it have gone badly. Thank your interviewers for seeing you, remark what a pleasure it was to make their acquaintance and sign off with a winning smile.

If no mention has been made of how to claim expenses, this is a matter that you could bring up with the secretary or receptionist. If she is uncertain of the procedures, note down your expenses on a piece of paper together with your name and address.

Coping with other selection procedures

Selection by interview is an imperfect method and some organisations rely on a whole battery of procedures to choose employees, some of which could last days if taken all together. Such procedures can be both exhaustive and exhausting, and the importance of being fresh and alert when you approach these sessions cannot be stressed too highly.

They include:

- **tests** to measure ability, general intelligence, aptitude, special aptitudes, trainability, attainment, personality, etc.

- **group exercises** to ascertain your capacity to get on with others, to influence others, to express yourself verbally, to think clearly and logically, to apply yourself to new problems based on past experience, etc.

- **essays** to find out if you can express yourself clearly and logically.

Some of the written tests take the form of a **multiple choice questionnaire**; others might involve **problem solving** or **drafting a report or a letter**. In all cases you need to work methodically through the test, disregarding those questions you can't answer first time round, and leaving time to check your answers at the end.

The group exercise might well be in the form of a discussion where each candidate takes the chair in turn, and attention is focussed on how you manage the discussion and relate to the others. Candidates are usually informed in advance as to what form these selection procedures will take.

WHAT TO DO AFTER THE INTERVIEW

After the interview or other selection procedure the candidate usually experiences a sense of anti-climax, and returns home feeling he or she could have done a lot better. However, it is worth bearing in mind that appointments are not made solely on the basis of an interview. Other factors are taken into account, such as your experience and the reports of your referees.

Some people, by contrast, leave the interview room quite elated believing that they have acquitted themselves with distinction. Yet at the end of the day it is the selector's opinion, not your own, which matters, and an over-confident attitude will not necessarily impress the selectors. All will be revealed in good time.

The initial meeting may just be a weeding out process, with the real business of selection left until the second occasion. On that second occasion you are in a stronger position, since much of the competition has been eliminated, but you cannot afford to relax. Repeat the preparations you made for the first interview, but much more thoroughly.

There are two practical steps to be taken in the 24 hours following the interview:

● Make notes of how you feel the interview went, the questions that you were asked and your impressions of the firm.

● Write a brief letter thanking the selectors for seeing you and confirming your continued interest in the position.

CASE STUDIES

Angela's lack of experience
Angela is somewhat apprehensive about being interviewed, but this is

something she will need to get used to. However, she takes a pride in her appearance and expresses her thoughts clearly, so she should make a good impression. To steady her nerves she should find out if her school can offer her coaching in interview techniques.

Bob's need to be businesslike
Bob has had some experience of being interviewed — for university, for example. He deals intelligently with any questions he is asked and does well in selection tests. However, he might put off some prospective employers with his long hair and tendency to arrive late. Bob could pick up some useful tips on job interview techniques from manuals in the library of the college Careers Advisory Service.

Colin has the tables turned on him
Colin is used to interviewing but not to being interviewed, so he must avoid turning the tables on his interviewer and subjecting him to scrutiny. He must be prepared to answer detailed questions on his experience and current responsibilities, and he might be asked to explain why he wishes to move on after quite a number of years with his present firm. Colin is the kind of person who might take exception to probing questions and would need to find ways of subduing his prickliness.

Doreen strengthens her hand
Doreen is used to handling people and expressing herself, as all successful mothers are — she should be able to take an interview in her stride. However, she has noticed that a local college runs a self-assertiveness course for women, and it would do no harm for her to enrol for this. The interviewer may wonder if her household chores and family responsibilities would affect her performance at the workplace, and she must have a convincing answer up her sleeve.

Edward's need to 'think young'
If Edward applies for another job he is likely to be older than many of the other candidates and possibly the interviewer(s) as well, so he must try to appear younger than he is and more alert. He should avoid sentences like 'in the old days we used to. . .' or 'I can remember a time when . . .'.

He needs to show that he is really conversant with modern practices and technology. Perhaps he could get a friend to interview him and have the interview videotaped to see where his weaknesses lie (including outdated mannerisms). A new suit would help to accentuate an up-to-date image.

10 Trident Close,
Much Landing,
Hants ML1 2XX

1st December 19...

Jim Short, Esq.,
Personnel Officer,
Tornado Aviation Services,
737 Boeing Way,
London DC10 3AA

Dear Mr Short,

Just a note to say how much I enjoyed meeting you yesterday at the interview, and to confirm my continued interest in the job.

May I thank both you and your colleagues for taking so much care over my application. I hope you will come to a speedy conclusion as to my suitability, and look forward to hearing from you.

Yours sincerely,

A.V.A. Torr

Fig. 8. Post interview letter.

9
Dealing with a Job Offer

You may be feeling frustrated because you have not felt really in control of events. But the moment you receive a letter or a telephone call offering you a position, you will once more be in command.

You might even find yourself faced with a problem: two job offers, though this is the kind of problem that most people can live with quite comfortably. Far from complicating matters this would simply extend your range of options to three: to accept Job Offer 1, to accept Job Offer 2 — or to turn both offers down.

Reject a job offer? The third option may sound perverse, particularly if you have been kicking your heels waiting for a positive reply. Yet all that glitters is not gold, and you need to consider carefully whether the offer makes sense in the context of your long term aspirations.

MAKING UP YOUR MIND

Let us deal with the positive news first of all. You have convinced people of your suitability for a particular post, and the decision-making ball is at last in your court.

One of the key principles of effective management is not to make hasty decisions. The organisation which has made the offer would really like an immediate response from you, but you are quite within your rights to ask for time to think things over, especially if the position is a fairly senior one.

During this period you can contact other organisations to find out how your other applications are faring. The fact that you have a job offer will show to them that you are a 'hot property' who is in demand, so if they want to take up their option on you they must act swiftly.

Is the offer acceptable?
Even if there is no other job offer in sight, you should weigh up your

new situation with care. What information have you received from the organisation? How does it compare with the impressions you gained from your visit? Then ask yourself the following:

- **Is the salary acceptable?** Is the firm offering me the rate for the job? Is the salary package sufficient to enable me to meet my commitments? Is it likely to rise in regular increments?

- **Is there a good working atmosphere?** What are the working conditions like? What are the staff like? Are they people that I can get on with?

- **Are the career prospects good?** Is the firm going places? What are the prospects for promotion? What facilities are there for career development?

- **Does the organisation enjoy a good reputation?** How is the organisation regarded by others, particularly its clients? How does it compare with its competitors or similar organisations?

- **Will the move cause disruption?** Will I need to relocate? If so, does the firm offer a relocation package? Will a move cause problems for my family? Will it affect my social life?

- **Does the job fulfil my career objectives?** Is this something that I really want to do? Or will it enable me to achieve my goals at some time in the future?

You should also be prepared to sound out friends and colleagues. They will have a shrewd idea of what you are capable of and happy to give you their opinions as to the advisability of your accepting the offer.

Consulting your family

Your dependents should also have their say, especially if they are going to be affected in some degree by your new job. This would happen, for instance, if you needed to relocate.

How would your spouse feel about a move? This is the age of the dual career family and if you are offered a job in Belfast you have to consider what effect this would have on your spouse who may well have a good job in Basildon and be reluctant to leave it.

A move could also have a disruptive effect on the education of your children. This is not really a problem if they are in primary school or at a boarding school; but to move them from one school to another in a year when they face crucial examinations should be avoided if at all possible.

An alternative strategy is not to move your home and family, but to find lodgings or a bachelor pad near your workplace where you stay during the week, and return home for the weekend. Thousands of people already arrange their lives in this manner, and although it could turn out to be a more expensive option, it could offer certain advantages.

Evaluating the contract

You cannot make any decision on the basis of inadequate information. Before you take a job you must be sure of the terms and conditions under which you will be employed. You therefore need to know:

- Name and address of the company
- Job title (with job description and grade, if applicable)
- Location(s) of work
- Date of commencement of employment
- Probationary period, if applicable
- Remuneration (including how increases are assessed)
- Pay interval (*eg* weekly, monthly)
- Hours of work and normal working hours
- Overtime arrangements (if applicable)
- Holiday entitlement and pay
- Pay arrangements during sick leave
- Period of notice required on either side
- Disciplinary procedures
- Grievance procedures
- Pension scheme, if applicable
- Redundancy terms
- Length of contract (if fixed term)
- Conditions of employment relating to trade union membership, if applicable.

Perks

Many companies offer their staff a number of extra perks, particularly senior staff, and you should enquire what these are. There are a number of possibilities, though it is highly improbable that any organisation will offer all of these:

- Employee share option scheme
- Bonus/profit sharing scheme
- Clothing or equipment allowance
- Private health insurance
- A company car
- Relocation allowance
- Sports and social facilities
- Subsidised canteen or luncheon vouchers
- Discounted goods
- Training allowances
- Counselling
- A children's creche
- Low cost loans
- Free travel

Generally speaking the smaller the company the fewer the perks. However, that should not be a disincentive. You will have more chance of making your mark in a small company, and a small firm may one day grow into an enormous corporation. Even if it does not, big is not always beautiful.

NEGOTIATING THE CONTRACT

If you decide not to take the job, tell the personnel officer as early as possible, preferably in writing, along the lines of the letter suggested in this chapter. This is the least you can do after they have spent so much time processing your application and interviewing you.

If you decide to accept, it is advisable to telephone the firm at the earliest opportunity and follow up the call with a courteous letter. Make sure you hand in your notice to your current employers in good time and try to part on the best of terms. After all, you may need to call on them for help again one day.

After considering the offer, you may have some reservations about it or want clarification on certain matters. If so, do not hesitate to get in touch with the firm, explaining that while you are positive about the offer, you would appreciate a discussion on some of the finer points of the proposed contract.

If you have been promised certain conditions in the interview, these should be clearly stated in the contract, since verbal agreements have no reliable legal standing. Do not ask for too much, but do not be afraid to make a few reasonable demands. You are, after all, in a strong position. The organisation clearly wants you and is anxious to make a good impression on you at the outset.

Do not list your demands over the telephone as this can convey a poor impression. The danger is that the organisation could decide to withdraw its offer and give the job to the reserve candidate. Make it clear that you want the job, and mention that you hope these minor matters can be resolved. The more senior the post the more likely it is that your employers will accede to your requests.

What is negotiable?

You may be unhappy with some of the conditions laid down. In which of the following areas do you feel your prospective employer would be most likely to grant your request? See page 183.

- Location(s) of work
- Date of commencement of employment
- Remuneration (including how increases are assessed)
- Holiday entitlement and pay
- Period of notice required on either side
- Pension scheme, if applicable
- Redundancy terms
- Conditions of employment relating to trade union membership
- Private health insurance
- A company car
- Relocation allowance
- Training allowances
- A children's creche

Clearly you should not push for too much in the initial stages — unless you are a very senior and experienced person — or the employer may decide to withdraw the job offer.

A WORD OF WARNING

Your hunt may be over for the moment, so you have cause for celebration. But a word of caution is in order too:

- **although you may have landed a 'permanent' position, no job can be deemed truly permanent these days.**

For instance, you may have to work for a probationary period before you are confirmed in the job. Your new organisation may experience a downturn, in which case as the last employee to be appointed you are likely to be the first to go.

Alternatively the job you so wanted could turn out to be a nightmare; for the sake of your sanity you feel the need to get out before much time has elapsed. You would be wise not to throw all your job hunting papers in the fire until some months have elapsed.

Even if all is well, there will be plenty of adjustments to be made when you get down to work, so you cannot afford to take things for granted. Indeed, if you intend to *manage* your career properly from now on this will be the precursor of other career moves.

CASE STUDIES

Angela gets two offers
Angela has received two job offers — one with a small local company which has limited prospects, and another with a large national concern in Birmingham which would involve her moving away from home. Then there is Uncle Quentin and his insurance company. Angela has no dependents so a move would not be disruptive; besides the job in Birmingham offers good prospects for advancement. This would appear the better option.

Bob — a bird in the hand
Bob only received one job offer and although it is not quite what he wanted, he decided to take it in case nothing better turned up. This could be a shrewd move because he will gain experience of the world of work and so increase his value in the eyes of employers. The job may turn out better than he expects, but if it does not, he does not have to stay on with the firm indefinitely. There is no reason why Bob should not continue his job search — albeit at a less intensive level, with a view to moving on after a couple of years.

Colin's quandary
Colin has received a job offer which he is seriously considering. The salary is marginally better than the one he is receiving from his current employer. Also, the post offers more responsibility, though Colin has a few doubts about the financial stability of the firm that wants him. He is wondering whether to mention the job offer to one of his superiors? If his current employers are keen to keep him they might come back with a tempting counter offer; yet in terms of Colin's long-term job strategy it would be better to move on. In a few years he will be less mobile and less willing to take risks; besides, he is

29 Verdi Crescent
Hull HU97 0YY

4th June...

Mr D Scarlatti,
Personnel Manager,
Donizetti Consultants,
20 Puccini Street,
London WC3 4XX

Dear Mr Scarlatti,

I am writing to thank you for offering me a position with your organisation. I am delighted to confirm my acceptance of this offer.

I very much look forward to working with you to ensure the continued success of the firm. As I mentioned in my interview I shall be free to commence duties at the beginning of September.

Please let me know of a convenient time when I can call in and finalise arrangements for my appointment.

Yours sincerely,

Indira Patel

Fig. 9. Letter accepting a job offer.

29 Shanghai Crescent,
Perth PH2 7YZ

4th June 19...

Mr D Scarlatti,
Personnel Manager,
Donizetti Consultants,
20 Puccini Street,
London WC3 4XX

Dear Mr Scarlatti,

After much consideration I must regretfully decline your kind offer of a position with your organisation.

The fact is I have just been offered an excellent job by another firm which offers greater scope for me to advance in my chosen career.

May I express my warmest thanks to you for all your kindness towards me, and may I wish you and the firm every success in the future. I shall watch your progress with great interest.

Yours sincerely

Kim Lee

Fig. 10. Letter rejecting a job offer.

most unlikely to be promoted to a top job if he stays in the same firm all his life.

Doreen has to choose

Doreen has been accepted for two jobs — one with a large organisation where she feels she would be a small cog in a large wheel, the other with a small company near home where the staff seem very friendly and she would enjoy a wide range of tasks. Doreen has decided to take a job with the latter because she feels she will be able to work better in a smaller tightly knit unit, and the management are prepared to be flexible in giving her time off to attend to household matters. Later, when she has found her feet, she might consider moving on.

Edward's charity

Edward has received a job offer from a medium-sized charity. The salary is lower than the one he now receives (usually the case with voluntary organisations) and the administration is somewhat chaotic. On the credit side it is a prestigious organisation which would offer new challenges and he would be making a valuable contribution to a cause he believes in. On the debit side, it would involve a great deal of travel and Edward doubts whether the job offers much security. He decides against taking it.

10
Getting Down to the Job

Landing a job is one thing; being a success in that job is something different. Your chances of acquitting yourself well will be helped if you start off on the right foot.

If you are moving from one job to another and are not too desperate to receive your first pay cheque, try to take a break of at least a week. You can regard this as a reward for your achievement in advancing your career, but it also serves a more serious purpose.

- You need to distance yourself mentally from your previous position. You could feel disorientated if you finish one job one day only to start another the next.

- You need to recharge your batteries. Starting a new job is a demanding process and you need to be at your most alert in the initial stages.

- You may need to prepare yourself for your new responsibilities. If your new job is not precisely the same as your old one, you may have to update your knowledge or skills.

PREPARING FOR YOUR NEW JOB

Before your holiday, see if you can spend a day or so with your new employers familiarising yourself with their business and procedures and clearing up contractual matters.

If you stumble across techniques with which you are not familiar or areas where you have become somewhat rusty, make a note of them; head for your nearest bookshop or library in search of relevant reading matter. You may startle your fellow holiday-makers when you sit on the beach at Corfu reading *Cost Control in the Metallurgical Industry*, but such preparation will stand you in good stead.

Should you have a particular weakness in any area of your new work, you could instead take a crash course to improve your knowledge. Contact a local college, your professional institute or trade union for advice on the type of training available. Alternatively, the organisation you have joined may well have its own staff training scheme that it will want to put you through.

There may be a delay of some months before you will be required at post. If you are not currently employed, you might look around for a temporary position to keep you busy and your bank manager happy and to get back into some kind of daily routine before you start your new job in earnest.

Getting to know the organisation

Organisations can differ greatly in the way they operate. Work practices you have followed elsewhere may be inappropriate in your new surroundings. For this reason many large organisations hold induction sessions for their new employees.

Induction

A comprehensive **induction** or **orientation** would include most of the following items:

- the organisation, its history and development
- the general nature of the work to be done
- company rules and safety measures
- employee benefits and services
- a detailed description of your duties
- how your job fits in with others in the department/firm
- introduction to key people you will be dealing with in the firm
- opportunities for career development
- conditions of employment (if not covered when you signed the contract)

A smaller firm will have less elaborate procedures: your 'induction' might just take the form of a brief chat with your immediate superior. If you are moving into a senior post you may fare even worse, because it may be thought superfluous to tell a senior person how things are done. If you were smart enough to get the job surely you know all there is to be known?

While it is flattering to have so much confidence placed in you from the outset, sooner or later you will come down with a bump. You might unwittingly offend a colleague by failing to consult, ruin the photocopier because you press the wrong button, or lose a contract because you do not follow the correct procedures.

While you can learn a great deal from your mistakes you are hardly likely to inspire confidence in your superiors if you appear accident prone. To manage your career effectively you need to be properly informed — not only when applying for a job but also when applying yourself to the job.

Therefore if no orientation seems forthcoming, you should ask for one, pointing out that it is in the best interests of everyone that you should be shown the ropes. The absolute minimum you need to know is:

- Who am I directly responsible to? (immediate superior)
- Who am I responsible for? (subordinates, clients)
- What are my duties? (job description)
- Where do I carry out these duties? (department, location)
- How does the equipment I may have to use work?
- When and how am I paid? (monthly? by direct debit?)
- Who do I see if I have a problem? (supervisor? shop steward? personnel officer?)

Mentoring
Some well organised firms may appoint a mentor who will act as your guide and helper in the initial stages. However this is by no means a universal practice and for many newcomers it is a case of 'sink or swim'. Whatever the arrangements, you will need to keep your wits about you at the start of your new job.

Finding out for yourself
No matter how good the orientation is, it will not cover everything. Those giving the orientation will want to give a good impression and may fail to draw attention to any shortcomings in the organisation, and may even be unaware of them.

For instances, the organisation chart may turn out to be somewhat idealised. It may show individual positions within the hierarchy, but not always indicate what the people in these posts actually do. The terms 'manager' or 'secretary' can mean any number of things; and you will need to find out who has authority to take decisions, not which job titles they hold.

You may well find that within the formal structure an informal network operates. Using this can cut corners and get things done quicker or more effectively than if you go through the normal channels.

You will doubtless have been told what is expected of you in your initial briefing, but these instructions may have only a tenuous link with reality. Look on your first days in a new organisation as a period of observation. Assume the mantle of a social anthropologist and seek answers to questions like:

● What do people wear? — Pin stripes or casual? There may be an unspoken dress code.

● What rules are obeyed and which ones are taken less seriously? — Some organisations are very casual while others are strict as to what you should or should not do.

● How do people in similar positions to your own behave? — It might be wise at first to adjust to the behaviour patterns of others.

● How hard do people work? — Is there a competitive atmosphere in the organisation or do people work at their own pace?

● How do people relate to one another? — Do they socialise much out of work? Are there tensions between certain individuals? Is there a pecking order?

● Who really rules the roost? — Who takes the decisions? Whose judgements are valued? A person's job title is not always an indication of this.

● What precisely is expected of you? — You may have been given a detailed job description, or just a vague idea of your duties. It could take a little time for you to find out what your tasks really are.

Understanding the corporate culture

If you live or travel abroad you cannot fail to become aware of national differences in behaviour and attitude. Germans are generally formal while Spaniards are informal; the Swiss are generally punctual, whereas the Portuguese are not; Arabs mostly tend to be demonstrative, the Japanese less so. Each country has its distinctive culture, defined by Geert Hofstede as 'the collective programming of the mind which distinguishes the members of one human group from another'. [1]

Organisations too have a culture all of their own. Sometimes differing cultures come into conflict as happened when two UK building societies tried to merge in 1993. To the outsider one building society seems much like another, but in this case the differences in ethos between the two firms were found to be so great that it was decided that a merger would cause more problems that it would solve. Negotiations were terminated.

Just as the culture of a country has an impact on the people who live there, so the culture of the organisation you work for will influence the way you work and act. Management theorists have identified four main types:

- Autocracy — 'We'll do it this way.' Decisions are taken at the top and you are expected to comply with them. There is little opportunity for discussion.

- Bureaucracy — 'We're supposed to do it this way.' Each person is assigned a well defined role, the organisation is stable and resistant to change. You progress slowly up the ladder.

- Technocracy — 'It's best to do it this way.' The work is task orientated. You are assigned to a succession of jobs or teams. A very flexible kind of organisation.

- Democracy — 'Let's do it together'. An organisation with little formal structure which serves to assist the individuals within it (*eg* a legal partnership).

Corporate culture and the individual
Any of us may thrive in one type of culture and fail in another. Which of the four categories would the following types of people prefer Compare your answers with those suggested on page 185.

1. Someone who is looking for security.
2. Someone who is keen to be involved in making decisions.
3. Someone who likes precise instructions.
4. Someone who likes to work independently.
5. Someone who likes to see his efforts bring results.
6. Someone who hates taking on responsibility.
7. Someone who hates change.
8. Someone who adapts easily to new situations.
9. Someone who admires firm leadership.
10. Someone who prefers a structured environment.

Getting on with colleagues

During your first days and weeks in a new job, do resist the temptation to upset the applecart. You may be amused by some of the practices you notice in your workplace, but do not dismiss them out of hand without first investigating the reasoning behind them.

Even if you have been appointed to a senior position and are keen to make an impact, your first task must be to acquire an in-depth understanding of how the organisation functions, not to sweep away one set of procedures and replace them with ideas of your own. The latter may have worked well elsewhere but in the present context they may be utterly inappropriate.

To achieve your aims and make progress in your career you will need to work with people. Let us consider them:

Your immediate colleagues
You will need to win their approval, but not by trying to outshine them. Be cooperative and friendly — but not too friendly. They will probably play the major role in helping you to settle in, and their advice — however weird it may sound — will have some validity.

Your superiors
Some bosses like to have frank and open discussions with subordinates; others expect them to be deferential. The trouble is there is no telling which kind you have, and initial impressions can prove false. In order to avoid open confrontation in the early stages of your employment, you should tread warily and defer.

Your mentor
In some companies there is a mentoring system for junior employees where one person is assigned to look after your progress within the firm and help you over any initial difficulties. In Japanese companies a mentor can play a vital role throughout a person's career. He or she acts as coach, protector, counsellor, role model, sponsor, friend and confessor, but in the UK the role tends to be much more limited. Try to find out what your mentor can and cannot do for you.

Your subordinates
Today's employees are much better educated and more sophisticated than their predecessors of half a century ago, and they no longer take kindly to newcomers who dictate to them. Why should they? — they doubtless know the job better than you. Rather than be haughty and

aloof you need to take an interest in your subordinates and communicate effectively with them. By earning their respect and trust you can develop a sound working relationship.

Your clients or customers
No matter how junior your position, when dealing with a client you represent the organisation you work for. These days most organisations claim to be customer-led (*ie* the customer's needs take precedence over everything else), though the reality may be different. Be charming and helpful to your clients. But for them you would not have a job!

YOUR PERIOD OF PROBATION

For the initial period in your new job you may be on probation. In other words the employer is trying you out to see how well you do the job and fit in with the organisation before confirming you in your position.

However, the probationary period is mutual. While your employer is observing your progress, you should be deciding whether the job or the organisation really suits you or whether you should consider moving on.

Towards the end of the initial period your immediate superior or your mentor may call you in to review your progress and decide on your future. During this session you may well get feedback on your work so far and be asked for your views of the organisation and whether you wish to continue.

Be prepared at this time for a frank and wide-ranging discussion. Think back to Chapter 2 where you sought to define your objectives. Consider now whether you have achieved them or will have an opportunity to achieve them if you stay in this post. Your objectives could have changed in the light of experience.

Unless you have proved very incompetent, the organisation will normally offer you a permanent position at this meeting. After all, it would be an admission of failure on their part if you were to prove unsuitable. If you are offered a more permanent contract, remember that the decision is yours.

Do not feel obliged to stay on indefinitely. If you feel ill at ease in your present employment, you may feel even worse in six months time, and it would be wise to cut your losses and resign at the earliest opportunity. Career management can involve you in hard decisions, and this is one of them.

CASE STUDIES

Angela settles in
Angela is a good learner and should settle down easily. Her employer is used to handling school leavers and assigns special staff to supervise their training. However, after a time she may well find that the job has certain drawbacks, and will need to reassess her objectives.

Bob's induction as a graduate
Bob can look forward to a well structured induction period. During this time he will be taken round the different departments of his new firm. There is a very competent graduate training officer who will act as his mentor (and for the others on the intake) and he will give Bob a confidential assessment of his prospects within the firm in a few months' time.

Colin's chaotic new environment
Colin's experience so far was in a somewhat structured environment in a firm which was solid rather than adventurous. He finds it something of a shock to be in a place which is pulsing with energy and the management structure is somewhat unclear. Things might have been less confusing if he had been through an induction session, but his employers felt that a person at his level of experience would not need one.

Doreen asks for help
Doreen is anxious to make a success of her new job and would benefit from having someone she can turn to for advice in the initial period. She has explained her requirement to the manager and he has promised to ask a woman of Doreen's age to take her under her wing.

Edward — taken for granted?
Edward would feel happiest in a 'democratic' type of firm which allows him to get on with things in his own way. Because of his seniority he is unlikely to be offered more than an introductory chat at any firm he joins. His colleagues and superiors, who could well be younger than he is, may be hesitant to offer him advice. Adjustment could prove tricky, but Edward's long experience in different organisations and departments should enable him to win through.

1 *Culture's Consequences*, Geert Hofstede (Sage 1984).

11
Moving Up and Moving On

REVIEWING PROGRESS

Once you have secured a position and settled down to your new job you may feel that there is little more to be done — that from now on your career will manage itself. You may be fortunate, particularly if you are a bright young management trainee, and find that your progress is carefully planned and charted by the personnel department. However, few organisations have the resources to look after you in this way.

Every so often — initially every six months and thereafter every year — you need to take stock. Some well regulated organisations conduct annual **staff appraisals** at which your mentor or immediate superior

- reviews your progress
- identifies problems and endeavours to solve them
- advises you on how you can improve on your current performance
- makes recommendations regarding your future.

Although such sessions are regarded with some trepidation, you can benefit enormously from the feedback you receive.

If you do not receive a regular appraisal you should certainly conduct one of your own, asking yourself the following questions:

- What did I set out to achieve?
- Have I achieved it? If so, how? If not, why not?
- What should I do next?
- What kind of preparation do I need?
- What criteria can I use for judging if I have succeeded?

106

KEEPING UP THE MOMENTUM

An essential element in career management is to keep up the momentum. If you start to coast along in your job — performing the same routine tasks and meeting no fresh challenges — it can have serious consequences for your career and general well-being. Let us consider what happens.

● You get stale. Instead of approaching each new task with fresh eyes you function on auto-pilot.

● You get bored. You cease to have any interest in or enthusiasm for the work. Overfamiliarity stifles your creative process.

● You get complacent. You get delusions of grandeur and assume that you are indispensable. You no longer take sufficient care with your work.

● You get taken for granted. You are asked to do the humdrum jobs that no-one else wants to do.

To summarise, your work suffers and so does your life style. So does the organisation that you work for, since no business can thrive if its staff are only half 'switched on'.

The need for stimulus

To stay in one place for far too long can stifle your creative process. 'Knowledge workers' need to be creative. Changes of environment are vital for scientists and engineers, for example, otherwise their powers of invention and imagination will decline.

It has been suggested that the optimum number of years for a research scientist or engineer to keep working in a field is that person's age divided by six or seven. Such a formula is intended to balance the need for freshness against the need for familiarity.

This principle could well encompass other professions. Computers and robots are taking over so many run of the mill functions, leaving tasks which require brainpower and creativity to human beings. If we follow the formula, a person in his twenties would stay in one place or department for four years; a person in his mid forties would move on after seven or eight years.

People at the beginning of their careers tend to be fairly mobile.

Working in different departments or organisations is an excellent way of gaining vital experience. However when reaching the late thirties and forties the rot sets in and many people try to stay in one place.

There may be good reasons for this. If you are a family man or woman you may want to stay put for the sake of your children's education. While the interests of your family deserve consideration, you should not abandon any idea of career progression. In a changing world it is essential to keep moving. The question is not 'whether to?' but 'in which direction?'

MOVING UP

Most people hope that one day their efforts will be recognised by promotion. In bureaucratic organisations like the armed services there may be as many as ten layers of seniority. People therefore expect to reach grade X in so many years. If they have not reached grade Y by the time they are forty-five they feel they have missed the boat or something has gone wrong.

Promotion acts as a stimulus. The employee has something to aim for, usually in terms of greater responsibility and a higher salary. However, the system can engender false hopes, as not everyone can rise to become chief executive. Indeed, many chief executives are no longer company men who have worked their way up, but executives recruited from outside. There are even plans to recruit outsiders for top positions in the civil service.

Promoting people from within is not always in the best interests of the organisation. According to the Peter Principle expounded by Laurence J. Peter and Raymond Hull, 'in a hierarchy every employee tends to rise to his level of incompetence.' [1] In other words people are promoted from jobs which they do well until they reach a position where they are incapable of carrying out the work satisfactorily, and there they remain stuck. Many a true word is spoken in jest.

Another consideration is that organisational structures are changing. Today organisations are introducing much 'flatter' structures, with only three or four levels. This means that the idea of promotion every few years is quite out of the question. You would be at the top of a very short ladder in next to no time — and (to stay with this metaphor) if you try to climb higher you will fall off.

In such circumstances we need to dismiss the idea that the only objective of career management is to find your way to the top of a chosen pyramid.

How to win promotion

Here are a few suggestions as to how you should behave if you wish to advance your career — and some on how not to. Try to identify the ones you need to follow and check your answers with those on page 185.

Action	*Tick*
Be helpful to your superiors, peers and subordinates.	_____
Draw attention to the shortcomings of others	_____
Find ways to stand out from your peers and get known to your superiors.	_____
Get a reputation for getting things done.	_____
Refuse to handle difficult tasks.	_____
Demonstrate complete reliability.	_____
Learn to make a good presentation using all the relevant techniques.	_____
Make sure others take the blame for your mistakes.	_____
Avoid making tricky decisions.	_____
Carefully nurture your business friends and contacts.	_____
Never run down your colleagues.	_____
Criticise regularly what you perceive as shortcomings in the establishment.	_____

Moving sideways

Mr Z is a very satisfied employee. He joined a large blue chip company as an engineer, but over the years he has had the opportunity to move around first into personnel and now into marketing. Although essentially a one company man, he has enjoyed three careers so far within the same firm.

This was an enlightened policy on the part of his employers. Too often people are shunted into a particular function with the result that their field of vision becomes narrower. They become so set in their ways that even the suggestion of a move will terrify them.

If your ambitions to move up the ladder seem to be thwarted, why not try to move sideways within your firm? It is not such an impossible task. In technocratic types of organisation, for instance, people are moving between departments and teams all the time.

It is in the organisation's interest to have a workforce that is flexible, and you might indicate to your superiors that you are interested in moving into another field if a vacancy arises. If your employer conducts staff performance appraisals, this is the time to mention it. There are various moves you could aim for including:

● Transfer to another department or branch. Your function may remain the same but you would be dealing with different people and applying your skills in a different context.

● Job change. You move to a job within the organisation which involves different skills (*eg* from R & D into marketing, from finance into general management). In some cases retraining will be required.

● Secondment. You are hired out or lent to another organisation (*eg* a subsidiary or a sister company abroad). Banks sometimes second their managers to local enterprise boards or charities.

Moving around helps you to broaden your experience and improve your visibility (*ie* gets you noticed). Gaining international experience is particularly useful in a world in which business and government are taking on a regional and global dimension. In due course your breadth of experience could well be a decisive factor in gaining your promotion.

MOVING ON

A decade ago an American called John Sculley had reached what many would have regarded as the pinnacle of his career. He was the chief executive of a giant corporation (Pepsi Cola), and doing very well for himself from the financial point of view. But one day he decided to move — to a smaller company where he would enjoy less status, a potentially bumpy ride, but far more challenges.

His move may have caused surprise in some business quarters; another person in the same position would probably have played safe and stayed where he was. But Mr Sculley realised an important truth: he was in danger of getting stuck in a rut — albeit a very comfortable rut — and if he delayed he would not be able to get out of it.

Moving on to work for another organisation may sound a drastic step, but it is becoming the accepted norm these days, particularly for high fliers. Such a move often leads to a higher salary, more responsibility, greater visibility, wider experience and enhanced prospects. Rather than lying submerged in one company waiting for promotion, you are taking your career into your own hands and moving up in the world.

Moving on could even mean moving out of paid employment altogether to work even more profitably for yourself. Or you may decide to change career direction altogether. These options are dealt with in Chapters 16 and 15 respectively.

Deciding whether to leave

Moving from one organisation to another can be hazardous, so you need to be quite sure that this is a sensible choice. Ask yourself the following questions:

- Has my career so far lived up to my expectations? — Do I enjoy my work? Am I finding it worthwhile? How far does it reflect my initial objectives?

- Am I getting a good deal from my employer? — Am I being paid the going rate? Am I being given responsibilities or am I being landed with tedious routine tasks that others do not want?

- Am I gaining a wide enough range of experience? — Does my employer have a proper training or staff development scheme? Do I have the opportunity to tackle a wide range of tasks? Do I have the option of gaining experience of different departments?

- Am I making good progress in my career? — Am I moving up within the organisation or am I trapped in my present position for the foreseeable future? Am I getting favourable feedback? Are my qualities and skills recognised and appreciated?

- Does the job offer good prospects? — What sort of prospects are there for advancement? What financial benefits can I aspire to compared with those offered in other organisations and careers?

- Is the work challenging enough? — Am I stretched to the full or just coasting along? How stimulating is the work? Am I engaged on a number of varied tasks?

- Do I relish remaining in this career for the rest of my life? — Do I have any major regrets about branching out in this direction? Is the novelty likely to wear off eventually?

- Am I in an environment where I can flourish? — Am I surrounded by helpful colleagues? Are the working conditions good? Does the firm provide good support facilities (*eg* counselling, mentoring, career development)?

- Is this the right time to leave? — Should I wait for better opportunities to come along or until the work situation is more promising? Might I be a more attractive proposition to another employer when I have gained more experience?

DEVELOPING YOUR TALENTS OUTSIDE THE WORKPLACE

After reviewing matters you may feel that your present position is just about tolerable and your personal circumstances such that you cannot really contemplate moving on.

There is no need to feel trapped. Instead you might consider your job purely as a means to an end (an income) and seek self-fulfilment away from the work place, particularly if you are an older person. A milkman may become a mayor, an insurance clerk a JP, a postman a lay preacher, a caretaker the leading light in the local dramatic society.

Activities to consider

Here are a few activities that spring to mind. You may be involved in some of these already. You could either seek greater involvement or extend your range of interests.

Public life
You could consider standing for the local council — even Parliament, becoming a Justice of the Peace, becoming a school governor.

Volunteer work
This could involve raising money for charities, helping out with the disabled, counselling people at the Citizens' Advice Bureau.

Education for leisure
You might decide to improve your qualifications, learn a language for your next foreign holiday, improve your knowledge of art.

Sport
You might wish to play a greater role in your local hockey or rugby team (as a player or coach) or spend more time improving your golf handicap.

Cultural activities
You could play more important roles in amateur dramatic society productions, learn to play a new musical instrument, or play in a dance band.

Hobbies
You could turn your attention to your hobbies, such as gardening, stamp collecting, astronomy, bird watching.

Religion
All religious groups rely to a large extent on unpaid helpers as lay assistants, non-stipendiary priests, church wardens, Sunday School teachers.

The fact that your energies are being dispersed is not detrimental to your performance at the workplace. The stimulus from your outside interests will make you a more alert employee and a more versatile personality.

CASE STUDIES

Feedback for Angela
While Angela may hope to stay with her employer for a good many years she should not hesitate to move on in order to broaden her experience. Being a conscientious young woman she would appreciate feedback; regular performance appraisals are a must for her.

Bob's need to gain experience
Bob too must concentrate on gaining experience in a wide range of fields. With luck the management training programme he is on will offer him experience in several departments in the firm. It will also enable him to discover which part of the organisation he would feel most at home in.

A mid career crisis for Colin?
Colin needs to consider his position very seriously, if he wants to avoid 'mid-career crisis' in a few years' time. He needs to extend his

experience, and should make it known to his superiors that if no promotion is imminent he would like an opportunity to move laterally within the organisation — perhaps a secondment abroad. If this is not possible, Colin should seriously consider finding another employer.

Doreen feels restless

Although Doreen's inclination is to stay in one place she feels that she would like more responsibilities. If she does not act soon she feels she will be doing the same job in 20 years' time. Doreen is now considering doing a part-time course at a local college and if her employer is prepared to give her time off — or even subsidise her training — she might view matters in a different light.

Edward seizes the initiative

Edward feels he is in definitely a rut and getting all the jobs that other people have turned down. He also has an inkling that he will be pushed out of it one of these days during a 'downsizing' exercise on the pretext that the firm needs new blood. But why wait for the push? If a move is on the cards, then Edward should be the one in the driving seat to make it happen.

1   *The Peter Principle*, L.J. Peter and R. Waterman (William Morrow, N.Y. 1969).

12
The Learning Society

Taking charge of your career also means taking charge of your education and training. Do not regard the acquisition of a certificate as a signal that learning stops here. In a world where knowledge can quickly go out of date it is merely the end of the first stage of a lifelong process.

If you are just out of school or college this thought may cause consternation. After all, you have spent the best part of fifteen or even twenty years in education and feel you have acquired enough education to last a lifetime. Yet in a society where so many jobs are now knowledge-based no one can really afford to stop learning. Ignorance may be bliss, but it will not help you to advance in your chosen career.

The same applies if you are older. Academics and the clergy are encouraged to take the occasional sabbatical, while continuous professional development has become the norm for medical staff. Even hard-headed commercial organisations are prepared to spend cash on training, as managers have come to realise that their employees are their key resource and the efficiency of their organisations will be impaired if they are not properly trained.

OPPORTUNITIES FOR CONTINUING YOUR EDUCATION

In a world of change education needs to be viewed as a lifelong process. It is in your own interest to join an organisation which takes staff development seriously and is prepared to offer regular periods of training. The armed services are exemplary in this regard; the private sector is inclined to offer this to only a select few, so you may have to seize the initiative yourself.

If you have neither the time or resources to devote to full-time study, what about more flexible learning arrangements? Fortunately educational and training establishments are responding to demand by offering all sorts of part-time study opportunities (*eg* short courses, refresher courses, evening courses).

There are opportunities at all levels to acquire qualifications awarded by City & Guilds of London Institute, the Royal Society of Arts (RSA), the Business & Technology Education Council (BTEC) and various professional bodies. You can also study part-time for a degree: Birkbeck College in London has long specialised in this and universities and colleges of higher education throughout the UK now offer a part-time option for some of their courses.

Getting information

You can find out just what is on offer by checking directories of courses in higher and further education in your local reference library. Many libraries and Job centres also have **Training Access Points** which can offer guidance on course options open, and there is also the **Educational Counselling and Credit Transfer Information Service (ECCTIS) database**. Local colleges and careers offices are another useful source of information.

Home-based study: the pros and cons

Not everybody can attend an institution of learning on a regular basis, and this is where **distance-learning** institutions come into their own. If you live in a remote spot, or are nervous about exercising your grey cells again, this type of course deserves investigation.

Joining the Open University

Continuing education received a boost in the UK with the establishment of the Open University. This teaches its students by means of printed material, TV and radio programmes and tutorials.

Learning by yourself without the stimulus of colleagues can be a lonely business, and requires strength of purpose as well as the ability to organise one's study effectively. The Open University overcomes this problem to some extent by organising tutorials (face to face or by telephone) and residential courses in the summer for its students.

Other distance learning institutions

It is not the only institution to offer such opportunities: the Open College, professional associations, trade unions and correspondence colleges are also involved in distance learning. They prepare people for a wide range of examinations from GCSEs to high level professional diplomas and university degrees. A number of tertiary level institutions are now offering flexible training packages which include a distance learning element.

Correspondence colleges generally provide study notes and a personal tutor to whom you have to submit assignments on a regular basis for grading and comment. The study notes in most cases have to be supplemented by further reading, so for the more advanced sources it plainly helps to have access to a reasonable library and bookshop. If you have difficulty in obtaining books locally, some of the colleges can despatch them to you. This can be beneficial if you live in a remote location, such as the Outer Hebrides.

These colleges tend to be fairly flexible organisations; you are not tied to the academic year and can embark on a course at virtually any time. You can also work at your own pace, though if you are entering for an examination you will have to plan your timetable to a deadline.

Vocational or non-vocational education?

What subjects should you choose to study? You may decide to opt for subjects that interest you rather than those oriented towards a career. The former are designed to develop the intellect and the 'whole person'; the latter to prepare you for a particular type of work.

Look at the following subjects. Which ones do you feel would be primarily *vocational* in content?

Archaeology	English	International Relations
Business Studies	French	Journalism
Computer Studies	Garden Design	Law
Dentistry	History	Mathematics

For a discussion of the answers, please turn to page 185.

Some courses with a vocational ring about them also have a substantial theoretical content. A teaching course, for instance, may deal as much with educational theory as with practical teaching methods. It is not enough to know *how* to do things; you need to understand *why* they are done in a particular way.

Suggestions for the undecided

Technology
If you have a technological bent, you should seriously consider training in the new technologies. Here, there are often **conversion courses** available for people whose background is in other fields. There is a shortage of people with skills in computer science, electronics, and some engineering fields, which looks likely to last till the end of the century.

Languages
If you are considering working abroad or taking a job which will involve foreign travel, an intensive language course makes a lot of sense. Even if you are based in Britain companies need staff who are competent in modern languages so that they can operate effectively in export markets.

Spoken and written ability in French, Spanish and German, and to a lesser extent Italian, is likely to prove increasingly important by the year 2000. But do not overlook the more esoteric tongues, such as Russian, Arabic, Chinese and Japanese. As trading links with these countries increase, fluency in one of these could greatly improve your job prospects in the world of commerce — within far-sighted firms, at least.

Management
There is a lot to be said for acquiring a management qualification or at least updating your supervisory skills. Firms today expect much greater professionalism of their senior staff — and some of the better ones are even prepare to finance the cost of any course. An advanced management course could stand you in good stead, like — for example — some of the distance learning MBA (Master of Business Administration) courses. Accountancy is another skill which is much in demand.

Teaching and social work
Alternatively, if you feel you would like to pass on your skills to others, you could consider training as a teacher or lecturer. Schools and colleges in Britain are experiencing a shortage of specialists in maths, science, modern languages and craft skills and the burgeoning social services are desperately short of qualified staff.

MAKING IT HAPPEN

Funding your course
One matter which deters would-be students from embarking on a period of study is the cost of a course — not only in terms of fees and general expenditure, but also the income you may lose in order to set aside time for study.

A grant will help to offset your expenditure, provided you can get one. Generally speaking the younger you are, the more likely you are to be eligible for a grant from your local authority. Contact them while you are still in the early stages of applying for a course. The amount of grant a UK student receives is affected by parental income, and most students find they need to supplement their grant in some way (*eg* with a student loan).

There are awards to mature students, but these tend to be discretionary rather than statutory, and you will have to put up a good case for yourself. Further information about grants are given in various leaflets from the Department for Education. *The Grants Directory* may help you spot alternative sources of finance.

Young people should be aware of scholarships available from public and private bodies — the armed services, for instance. If you are in employment, your organisation may be prepared to sponsor you — there is no harm in asking. If all else fails and you have no private income on which you can exist, you can always try the bank. The UK Government has introduced a system of **career development loans** in cooperation with certain banks for people embarking on vocational training.

Overcoming study problems

Even if the financing of your course is assured, there is bound to be an element of self-doubt, especially if some years have elapsed since you last followed a course of study. Yet contrary to general belief you do not become less able to think and learn as you grow older. You just imagine you do.

At one time serious study after school and college tended to be the preserve of scholars and clergymen. Nowadays, people in all walks of life have embarked on challenging courses which they have completed with credit even though they are in their forties, fifties or sixties.

Further study should hold few terrors for younger people; they are used to learning. Older people may feel they are slower on the uptake but they have certain other valuable assets. If you fall into this category, your years of experience and fund of accumulated knowledge will more than compensate for the apparent quickness of the younger student.

This is not to say that your first few weeks of study will not turn out to be challenging. Indeed, you could well experience a feeling of inadequacy when confronted with a long reading list or a lecturer who seems to speak in riddles.

Writing an essay can be a daunting task if you have not needed to commit your thoughts and conclusions to paper for twenty years or more, but the problem is not lack of ability, just lack of practice.

Textbooks may seem quite frightening until you realise that they are not to be read in the same way as a Jeffrey Archer novel but have to be scanned for information, not consumed from cover to cover.

Don't despair. This is not a matter of having to learn new tricks, but rather of relearning the old ones. You have to regain the study habit and resort to those techniques which you picked up quite easily when younger.

If you think back, in your younger days you could have dealt with such problems in your stride. Even if you couldn't, there is no reason why you cannot learn appropriate learning strategies now. There are plenty of manuals available which can instruct you in learning techniques. some of the booklets published by the **National Extension College**, for instance, will help you get off to a good start.

Periods of study — part-time or full-time — should be regarded as an essential part of one's career development in a rapidly changing world. Moreover, winning a well regarded qualification will make you much more attractive to potential employers.

CASE STUDIES

Higher education for Angela?

Angela is an intelligent person who really ought to consider going on to higher education like one third of her contemporaries. After all, she has no obstacles in her path. If she takes an approved course, she will qualify for a grant from her local authority. If she puts it off till later she will find it more difficult to get back into the learning mode and may have other distractions.

But what can she choose? Her father has suggested a course in business studies (he would, wouldn't he), but Angela rather fancies studying art, though she cannot envisage what she will do at the end of the course. She needs to investigate the range of art courses available; those with a strong design component might prove particularly interesting.

Bob's options

If Bob wants to make himself more attractive to employers, he might investigate a vocationally oriented course, perhaps leading to a professional qualification from a professional organisation. The Institute of Chartered Secretaries or the Institute of Administrative Management would be possibilities. A postgraduate certificate in education is another, provided teaching appeals to him, and he should be eligible for a grant.

Bob has been thinking of doing a higher degree in history, which is fine if he plans to become an academic. However, competition is very keen and unless he is confident that he can secure a post at the end of his course he would do well to look at other possibilities.

Colin's great push

This is an ideal time for Colin to embark on a process of self-development. The thirties are the ideal time for that great push forward. If he is aiming to get to the top of the ladder in his forties, he needs to be in sight of a fairly senior position by the end of the decade.

Better qualifications could tilt the balance in his favour. He doesn't have an MBA, and as he is keen to get on in business, he should seriously consider studying for one. He has skills which could be in demand abroad, in which case he might consider doing a language course and getting a little international exposure.

Unfortunately, Colin has heavy financial commitments and cannot really afford to take a year off work, unless his firm will sponsor him. His studies will have to be on a part-time basis — probably evening classes or even distance learning with the Open University Business School.

Doreen as a 'returner'

Doreen may well find a course of study helpful. She could start by enrolling on a 'back to work' course for returners which would help her to clarify her aims. She is hesitant about enrolling for a full-time course but if she does she would want to study locally because of family commitments. Her best plan is to find out what is on offer from local education institutions.

Doreen's first priority is to get back to work, and one idea she has is to take a refresher course in typing or office management at the local college of further education. But in the long run she is looking for something a bit more challenging. Her children are likely to go on to university or college, and she would like to prove she is their intellectual equal.

Her first port of call should be the nearest tertiary college to see what kind of courses they offer. If there is nothing that appeals to her or it does not seem able to accommodate a part-time returner (funny, because they are a growing force in the land!), she ought to explore distance learning courses — with the Open University, for instance. The fact that she did not pass many exams at school will not prevent her doing a course with the OU.

Edward looks to the future

Edward is sceptical about starting a course at his age. 'You can't teach an old dog new tricks,' he barks. Yet, if he opts for self-employment enrolling for a part-time course on running your own business or marketing might be quite a sensible plan.

Another idea would be to look on education as a way to develop new interests for the next 25 years of his life — the Third Age. Edward is developing an interest in old clocks and would like to learn more about them. If he were to take a course with the Institute of Horology he could become a qualified clockmaker, a move which could ultimately lead into a second career.

13
Managing Problems at Work

Careers have their ups and downs even when they are properly managed. No manager however brilliant can expect a trouble-free ride. In the late 1980s famous entrepreneurs took their companies to new heights of profitability and it seemed that the sky was the limit, but in the recession of the early 1990s several of these came down to earth with a bump.

When everything is working in your favour, management is a smooth and relatively trouble-free process and we soon forget harsher times. But when tougher situations arise, hard decisions have to be made and success is no longer guaranteed. To manage an organisation or career effectively over the long term we have to be able to cope successfully when the outlook is less promising.

To enable you to become a 'manager for all seasons' this chapter and the next examine some of the difficulties you may meet and suggest ideas which could help to alleviate them.

MANAGING STRESS

How stressful is your work?
In 1993 the Institute of Management conducted a survey of managers and came up with some grim findings. 'It paints a graphic picture of men (and some women) under stress — shouldering ever-heavier work, clocking up long hours, often well beyond the call of contractual duty, taking work home, in some cases several days a week and every weekend, and suffering a variety of unpleasant consequences, ranging from headaches and chronic insomnia to alcohol dependence, sexual inadequacy, exhaustion and marital breakdown,' writes Peter Wilsher. [1]

Who would be a manager in such circumstances? And yet it is reckoned that top managers lead less stressful lives than many of their subordinates. Surely this does not bode well for British industry?

Few jobs are entirely stress-free, nor should we wish them to be: many of us are at our best when our adrenalin is flowing. The problem becomes serious only when you are exposed to excessive pressure over a long period. Recurrent stress could endanger your career, and instances are sometimes cited of high fliers who experience 'burn out' in their mid-thirties.

In a well managed career this kind of outcome can be avoided. Stress is normally caused by a combination of problems. One can try to cure it by medication, yoga, exercise, sleep or therapy, but first you should deploy your managerial skills to identify these problems, and then find solutions to them one by one.

Who experiences stress?

Some jobs are inherently more stressful than others. Look at the following jobs and try to rank them in terms of stressfulness, putting the most stressful first.

Publisher	Fireman	Dentist
Actor	Estate agent	Professional sportsman
Nurse	Bus driver	Miner
Vicar	Policeman	Librarian
Optician	Accountant	Doctor

For answers and comments please turn to page 187.

MANAGING YOUR HEALTH

Illness is sometimes stress-related but not always. All illnesses should be taken seriously: even a bout of influenza can greatly impair your efficiency. A recurrent illness or a bad accident could hamper your ability to do your job properly and damage your promotion prospects. Some larger firms insist on regular health checks, especially for senior staff. These enable long-term problems to be diagnosed at an early stage and remedial action taken before matters get out of hand.

Lifestyle can play an important role in maintaining good health. A sensible diet, abstemiousness, sensible hours and regular exercise are to be recommended. You could enrol for keep fit classes in an expensive health club but there are other much cheaper ways of taking exercise. Walking, swimming and gardening, for instance, are three very healthy activities.

MANAGING PERSONAL PROBLEMS

The family

You cannot insulate your job completely from your home life. If the baby keeps you awake all night you may feel decidedly below par at work next day. The death of a spouse or a divorce are two of the most stressful events a person has to contend with and are bound to affect your performance at work.

Be prepared to confide in others. Ensure that your superiors and colleagues are aware of the problems you are facing. They may come up with things to help you over the worst (*eg* a period of leave, revised work schedules, counselling, moral support).

If you are married with young children your responsibilities at home may clash with your duties at work. Discuss with your employers the possibility of a more flexible work pattern (job sharing, part-time work, working from home). If they value your contribution they may well agree. Some organisations provide workplace nurseries and childminding facilities, and this kind of provision is likely to increase in the future.

Personal relationships

If you do not get along well with your colleagues, your superiors or subordinates, life can become a misery. A number of firms have policies to deal with racial and sexual harassment at work, but there are various types of behaviour which are just as odious. Before you spring into action you should try to discern possible motives. Ask yourself the following questions:

1. Are you at fault? Are you uncooperative, snooty, surly or offhand? Are you failing to pull your weight or putting the others to shame?

2. Is there some misunderstanding? Are you trespassing on someone else's preserves? Is there some ambiguity about your actual position? Are people suspicious of you?

3. Is there someone who bears a grudge towards you? Is someone angling for your job? Does that person behave in the same way towards others?

4. Are you temperamentally unsuited to working with others? Would you feel happier working on your own? Do you get nervous in the presence of other people?

Managing personal relationships is a key factor in career success, so you should not allow a nasty situation to grow or fester. If the problems are caused by a particular individual — colleague, subordinate or boss — arrange to meet him or her in a non-confrontational situation to discuss what is wrong. Plan your approach carefully and try to visualise possible reactions to your words.

If a number of people are involved you should report the matter to your superior or the personnel department. If the matter cannot be resolved amicably you could ask for a transfer, a change in your working arrangements or — as a last resort — you could leave the job.

PATTERNS OF WORK

Overwork

Most work has its seasonal peaks and troughs, and during the peaks you may well find that you work longer hours. If this is happening all the year round, something must be wrong. Here are some questions for you to answer.

Are you delegating properly?
As you progress up the organisation you cannot take all your jobs with you; instead you must delegate them to others. Are you doing this? If the excuse is 'No, because no-one is capable of doing these jobs,' you should consider training people so that they do become capable.

Are you performing unnecessary tasks?
Keep a detailed diary for a few days to see what tasks you are performing and time how long each one takes. Are all these tasks necessary? If you are not sure, prioritise them. Can the low priority ones be ignored altogether?

Are you managing your time effectively?
List your tasks for your day (or week) and allocate each one a certain amount of time on your schedule. This way you stand a better chance of achieving all of them than if you take things as they come.

Underperformance

Poor performance may be another cause of overwork, but it deserves a section on its own since it can lead to stress and even dismissal. If you fail to perform satisfactorily, everyone suffers, and no organisation can afford to have a weak link. Before you can take remedial action you need — perhaps with the help of your mentor or immediate superior — to identify the cause or causes. Examples are:

Inadequate preparation for the job
To be placed in a position without adequate training or orientation is a recipe for disaster. In many modern work situations there is no room for trial and error, so you should request a proper induction or training — repeated if necessary.

Ambiguous goals
If you have no clear idea of what you have to accomplish you are less likely to achieve your goals. Ask for clarification of what you should be aiming for.

Insufficient ability
It is just possible that you have been promoted to your level of incompetence — The Peter Principle. Instead of trying to cover up, face up to your limitations: try to move sideways to a position where you can cope better, or see if the job can modified.

Underuse of skills
The work is neither stimulating nor challenging, so you get bored and drift along on autopilot. See if the scope of the job could be enlarged to make more effective use of your talents or look at the possibility of a job change.

Inadequate resources
You do not have enough tools or people of the right calibre with which to do your job. There is a danger that this could be regarded as an excuse to cover up your own incompetence, so try first to find ways to make more effective use of what resources you have.

Value conflict
You do not feel at ease in your job because it conflicts with your deeply held convictions (*eg* working on Sunday, doing something which you suspect is illegal). Explain your feelings to your superiors and see if they can find a solution. This kind of problem is quite common in a multicultural workforce where a manager from one culture does not understand the values of another.

Discrimination
Are you losing out in the promotion stakes? Are you getting all the

jobs no one else is prepared to do? If you are a woman or from an ethnic minority (or both) you may feel you are being discriminated against on the grounds of your sex or race.

But can you *prove* it? Before you raise the matter with your employers you need to be sure of your facts. Perhaps you have not raised the matter of promotion with your employers and they assume you have no ambitions; perhaps the people who are promoted are either better qualified or have worked for the organisation longer than you; or perhaps they fear that other employees will not be prepared to accept orders from you.

Have a discreet chat to your superiors or the personnel officer first of all. If you are dissatisfied with their response, consult with the nearest office of the Equal Opportunities Commission.

MANAGING UNCERTAINTY AND CHANGE

Career uncertainty

While some people are eternal optimists, most people at some time or other are beset by self-doubt and concern about the future. A number of factors can trigger anxiety:

- **Changes at the top.** Your boss leaves, and you wonder whether you will get along with his successor.

- **Changes in the organisational structure.** The organisation is restructured, sometimes in the wake of a takeover or merger. You wonder whether your job could be on the line.

- **Changes in the nature of the job.** You might be asked to take on extra responsibilities or an increased workload and you are uncertain whether you will be able to cope.

- **Recession.** Times of recession lead to increasing levels of unemployment. You fear you could become a casualty.

- **Mid-career crisis.** You feel stuck and no longer in charge of your destiny. You realise that various doors of opportunity have now closed and no others seem to be opening.

Rather than waiting for the heavens to drop, *take the initiative*. If you hear rumours of impending changes, ask your superiors if they are true. If so, ask what is the rationale behind them? Often suspicions are aroused unnecessarily because of poor communications within the organisation.

If you feel you may have to take on extra responsibilities, be positive about this and ask for training in your new duties. Be ready to suggest ways in which you could make a more positive contribution to the success of the organisation, particularly if it is going through a difficult patch.

At the same time keep your ear to the ground about possible redundancies and start exploring other career options if it seems that your job might go.

Be positive

If you cannot resolve these and other problems yourself, do not hesitate to seek advice. A number of larger organisations now offer **counselling** facilities to their staff with varying degrees of confidentiality.

If your problems emanate from outside your workplace, organisations such as **Relate**, the **Samaritans** and **Alcoholics Anonymous** are there to help you. Also the **British Association for Counselling** may be able to put you in touch with one of its members. You will also find courses offering therapy of different kinds at colleges and other institutions throughout the country.

We all experience problems at some time or another, and if you prove sympathetic to other people and their problems, you are more likely to have a shoulder or two to cry on when things go badly for you.

CASE STUDIES

Angela is surprised

Angela has not experienced many of the problems mentioned above, except for one or two colleagues who were rather abrupt with her. She bought one of them a mug of coffee in the staff canteen and discovered the woman was experiencing problems at home. Since then relations have improved.

Bob's run of bad luck

Bob has had a run of problems lately: a death in the family, a bust-up with his girl friend, a bad leg injury incurred while playing hockey and a transfer to a new department. He feels everything is getting on top of him and he is finding it hard to cope despite working a twelve hour day. Bob should inform his mentor of these difficulties, and see

if there are ways in which he can solve them (an in-service course on
time management, perhaps?)

Colin copes with his younger boss

Colin has no major problems at the moment, but he is finding his new
boss, who seems half his age, a pain in the neck. The boss comes out
with all sorts of new management theories which are virtually
meaningless to Colin and he wonders how much more he can take.
Before doing anything rash Colin needs to get to know the chap a bit
better — by inviting him for a pint down at the Green Dragon perhaps? It could be that the new man is nervous, anxious to show his
mettle, and has problems in developing a rapport with people.

Doreen hates pressure

Doreen's main problem has been adapting to a structured work environment after enjoying greater autonomy as a housewife. In the early
stages she sometimes felt out of her depth because things were not
explained to her thoroughly or she had to memorise a lot of written
instructions. She find she can learn well provided she is not too press-
urised and learns on the job.

Edward feels undervalued

Edward has been passed over for promotion and wonders if he can
appeal to a tribunal on the grounds of discrimination. (The answer is
probably not, but he should try to find reasons from his immediate
boss.) Increasingly Edward finds that his values differ from those of
his employer and he wonders whether he would thrive better in other
surroundings. It is not too late to seek guidance: an experienced counsellor would help to understand himself better, redefine personal goals
and reach decisions about the future direction of his career.

1   *The Mixed-Up Manager*, P Wilsher (*Management Today*, October 1993).

14
Managing Redundancy

You may be surprised to find a chapter in this book dealing with redundancy. 'Surely,' you say, 'if I am managing my career properly I will never find myself out of work?'

One of the messages in this book is certainly that prevention is better than cure. You should keep a close eye on emerging trends and if you have read the situation correctly you will not be taken unawares when redundancy notices are handed out. You will either have moved on or be well advanced in your search for new opportunities.

Yet even the most alert people are sometimes caught unawares, and this can be a really unnerving experience. If the axe falls on your job, you will experience a variety of emotions — shock, fear, anger, humiliation, guilt, depression, or perhaps even relief.

Panic is not an ideal state of mind to be in as you prepare to launch yourself on to the next stage of your career. However, your experience of career management should stand you in good stead even in these dark days. Redundancy is, after all, just another problem awaiting the correct solution.

TAKING CHARGE OF YOURSELF

Springing into action
Losing your job should not be regarded as a disaster, but rather as the prelude to new opportunities. The experience should liberate you and allow you to go after better things. The last thing you should be doing is spending time fretting when your redundancy notice comes through.

Instead, you need to make plans for the future bearing in mind that the ideal time to start looking for a new job is while you still have one. You will be a much hotter property in a prospective employer's eyes than someone who is on the dole.

You may have seen the writing on the wall some months previously but failed to act. You now need to spring into action with a vengeance in order to get ahead of the pack in the search for a new position.

There are various reasons for applying yourself to the job hunt before your current job peters out. While you are still employed you have a wide range of contacts inside your firm and also outside it, and you can use them to keep you informed of any opportunities that may be on offer in your particular field.

Even if your contacts cannot offer you job leads, they may be able to offer you ideas and encouragement — both of which you will miss when you have to go it alone from home. Most people find they are better motivated when surrounded by others, principally because there are people around them against whom they can bounce off ideas, and measure their job hunting progress.

Should you leave immediately?

In some cases you will be asked to leave immediately, which may seem harsh and abrupt, but from your point of view has certain advantages. It means you can concentrate on finding a position right away.

On the other hand if the whole organisation or department is being shut down you may be asked to stay on to wind up the operation, especially if you hold a senior position. Is there any point in making a final effort for an organisation which has decided to dispense with your valuable services?

There is indeed. Your conduct during the final stages of your employment could leave a lasting impression on your old bosses, and a good impression is much more desirable than a bad one. Remember, too, that you are going to need their help in the future . . . to provide references, for instance.

If you play your cards right, you could possible gain a number of favours from your old firm, and this should be one of your conditions for staying on to the bitter end. These might include:

● **Putting you in touch** with business associates or colleagues who are on the lookout for new staff.

● **Secretarial assistance** in your search for new employment.

● Redundancy **counselling** and job search help by professional outplacement consultants. *The Corporate Directory of Career Change and Outplacement* lists details of the leading ones. If such help is not apparently forthcoming, it does no harm to ask whether it might be, in the hope that a conscience might be pricked somewhere.

- Various **perks**. Some redundant executives are offered the opportunity to purchase their company car at a knockdown price, or at least keep it for their own use until the end of the financial year. There may also be a chance of keeping up contributions to the company pension scheme or other fringe benefits such as health insurance, low cost mortgages or life insurance. (In the case of company pensions you should seek professional advice: your age can have a considerable bearing on your best option, and it might be better to withdraw your funds and put them into a personal pension scheme. Large sums can be won or lost depending on which move you make and you should take appropriate advice.)

- A **golden handshake**. A generous redundancy settlement in excess of the statutory minimum is something you should aim for, particularly if you can point to a lengthy and distinguished record of service to an organisation which is still flush with cash. Such a payment should not be regarded just as a bonus. It is, in fact, designed to tide you over until you secure your next job (see **Redundancy Law**).

REDUNDANCY LAW

Notice of redundancy
You should get the amount of **notice** mentioned in your contract — normally not less than a week for over 4 weeks' and less than 2 years' continuous employment; and one week's notice for each year of service thereafter (maximum 12 years). Payment in lieu of notice is possible. This means you do not need to work out the period of notice but are paid for it.

You ar entitled to reasonable paid time off to look for training and work. The maximum amount of paid time off for which an employer is obliged to pay is two fifths of a week.

You must claim your redundancy pay within 6 months of leaving.

If you are guilty of a gross breach of contract (*eg* disobedience, dishonesty) you can be dismissed without notice.

Redundancy payment
In the UK in order to qualify for a redundancy payment you should be under 60 (women) or 65 (men) and have worked for the employer in question for:

- over 16 hours a week for 2 years or
- over 8 hours a week for the past 5 years

If you are on a fixed term contract these provisions do not apply.

Legal entitlement
The legal minimum varies according to age and length of service (maximum 12 years):

- 18-22 year olds: half a week's pay for every year completed
- 22-41 year olds: one week's pay for every year completed
- Over 41: one and a half week's pay for each year after your 41st birthday.

Unfair dismissal
If you believe you have been unfairly dismissed you may complain to an **Industrial Tribunal** within three months of dismissal. The onus is then on the employers to prove that they acted reasonably. If the tribunal finds against the employers it can:

- order that you be reinstated
- award compensation.

You normally have no legal redress if you are on a fixed term contract which is not renewed on termination. To find out more about this, see T. R. Naylor's book *How to Apply to an Industrial Tribunal* in this series. This explains how you can make your claim without having to use a solicitor.

The laws of redundancy are subject to change and apply only to the United Kingdom.

PUTTING YOUR FINANCES IN ORDER

Now that you have lost your chief source of income, your salary, you cannot be sure how long it will be before you receive your next salary cheque. Even the best managed job search can take months, and in the meantime you have to keep body and soul together.

A change in your circumstances can wreak havoc with your finances. You will need to take a long hard look at your financial situation to see what changes are needed to balance the books over an extended period. Do not delay.

Your expenditure

First, you need to work out your weekly or monthly expenditure. This will probably include:

- household expenses (food, utilities)
- mortgage repayments or rent
- council tax/rates
- personal transport (road tax, insurance, servicing)
- insurance and pension payments
- subscriptions, fees
- personal expenses (clothes, toiletries, *etc*)
- entertainment and social activities
- loan or credit repayments
- rental charges

Your income

Against this you need to set your anticipated income which would include:

Contributory benefits (notably, unemployment benefit) [1]
These are benefits that you are entitled to provided you have made enough of the relevant contributions. They are not generally affected by any other income you may have. However, if you have not paid enough **national insurance contributions** of the right type during the past two years you may not be entitled to it. You should make a claim at your Unemployment Benefit Office the first day you are out of work.

Means tested benefits
This includes for example income support, housing benefit, family credit. The amount you are entitled to depends on the value of your savings and other income. [2]

Investment income
For example from a building society or bank account, unit trusts, stocks and shares.

Insurance income
Assuming you are insured against redundancy.

Any earned income
For example from your spouse or from any part-time work you under-

PERSONAL BUDGET

Expenditure   £

Household expenses (food, utilities)   _____

Mortgage repayments or rent   _____

Council Tax/Rates   _____

Personal transport   _____

Insurance and pension payments   _____

Subscriptions, fees   _____

Personal expenses   _____

Entertainment and social activities   _____

Loan or credit repayments   _____

Rental charges   _____

Other   _____

TOTAL (Expenditure)   [_____]

Income
Contributory benefits   _____

Means tested benefits   _____

Investment income   _____

Insurance income   _____

Any earned income   _____

Pension   _____

Other income   _____

TOTAL (Income)   [_____]

Total surplus/shortfall   _____

Fig. 11. Budgeting your income and expenditure.

take. Under Social Security rules in the UK unemployment benefit is assessed on a daily basis. This means in effect that if you earn over a certain amount [3] on a particular day you forfeit your benefit for that day but still receive benefit for the days you do not work.

Pension
Now compare your anticipated income with your current expenditure to decide if you are going to break even. If your income exceeds your expenditure then you have nothing to worry about for the time being. But bear in mind that the jobseeker allowance is of limited duration.

If there is a shortfall, you will need to find ways of pruning your expenditure, which can be a painful process. Think of ways in which you could achieve this and compare your ideas with those in the Appendix.

Improving your financial situation
If you find that you are overcommitted financially and see no way of narrowing the gap between income and expenditure, see if you can get a better return from any investment or savings. If you have received a substantial redundancy payment, explore ways of investing it in a way which will provide a reasonable income. It should not be spent on a day at the races or a new Porsche!

If your situation looks very difficult, you could enlist the aid of the Citizen's Advice Bureau which offers a debt counselling service.

You could look into the possibility of doing part-time or seasonal work, but remember that you will need to declare your earnings to the Unemployment Benefit Office, and your allowance will be reduced accordingly for the days that you work.[3] Part-time or temporary employment might even lead to an offer of full-time employment.

Life between jobs can be an anxious period for everyone concerned, and it can be even more traumatic if it involves lurching from one financial crisis to another. Take stock of your finances and institute a régime of careful budgeting right from the start; you can then devote yourself with a clear conscience to what should be your primary concern: searching for your next job.

ESTABLISHING A NEW ROUTINE

Making a start
You may regard yourself as jobless, but in reality you have a very important task to perform, that of getting back into a job — unless you have opted for self-employment or a sabbatical.

It is all too easy away from the structured world of the workplace to sink into a state of torpor. Loss of status, anxiety about the future, lack of inter-personal contact and the feeling of rejection can cause people to crawl into their shells and feel sorry for themselves.

However, you should not waste your newly found freedom to forget the world about you and spend your days pottering about in the garden or watching television. Finding a new job may turn out to be a far more protracted process than you expected. Apply yourself to this task without delay. (See also Chapter 4, Planning your job search.)

Setting up your office

Set aside a room or a corner of your house for use as an office. You will need a desk or table, plenty of stationery, a typewriter or word processor, files for correspondence and job details, a day by day planner and a card index system.

Each index card is for recording the progress of a job application and should have the following headings

Details of position — including address and contact
Date of sending application
Date of receiving reply
Result
Date, place and time of interview
Result
Date, place and time of follow up interview
Final outcome
Comments

Making out a timetable

It is important to work out a realistic schedule for yourself. Here is an example:

9 am to 12.30:   Office. Deal with correspondence; prepare applications (letters, application forms, CV); update your paperwork.

2 pm to 5 pm   (Monday, Wednesday and Friday). Meet friends, chase up contacts — in person or on the phone, visit Job Centre, recruitment consultants, careers counsellor, *etc*.

2 pm to 5 pm   (Tuesday and Thursday). Visit Job Library or reference library to check jobs adverts and research companies and organisations that might be worth approaching.

The timetable will need to be flexible so as to cope with job interviews, visits to careers conventions or courses you may decide to take.

Setting yourself targets

One school of thought reckons that you need to make ten applications to secure one interview and ten interviews to secure a job offer (*ie* 100 applications in all). Though much will depend on the type of job you are after and the state of the jobs market it is a useful yardstick which should galvanise you into action.

Try setting down on paper the following weekly targets for yourself:

x replies to job advertisements
x speculative applications
x visits to recruitment consultants or companies
x telephone contacts

Every so often — at the end of every fortnight or every month — you should review your progress.

Keeping fit and healthy

It is only too easy to let yourself go physically and this can affect your mental state and general well-being. You should therefore allocate time in your schedule for regular exercise. This does not have to involve you in tremendous expense: if you walk or ride a bicycle everywhere you will actually save money, and these are two excellent ways of keeping in trim — swimming being another.

A fit person is an alert person and you will cut more of a dash with prospective employers if you appear to be in good shape.

Keeping your mind active

Read newspapers, books and professional journals; do crosswords and other puzzles that require mental agility; keep abreast of what is happening in your professional field; take a course; take an active part in a discussion group.

CASE STUDIES

Angela gets a nasty shock

Angela is shocked to be made redundant after such a short time in her first job and should check that this has not occurred because of any failings on her part. Unfortunately, when firms have to rein in, some operate on the 'last in, first out' principle — regardless of the quality of the person. Angela should arrange a discussion with the personnel officer or her mentor to see if the firm can offer any help in finding a new job.

Bob's relief

Bob's job has suddenly come to an end after a year because of restructuring within the firm. Since he does not like the job very much, he breathes a sigh of relief and wonders what to do next. Fortunately the firm has engaged the services of an outplacement consultancy to help redundant staff find new jobs. Bob should take full advantage of the in-depth careers counselling they offer which is paid for by the firm.

Colin gets angry

Colin suddenly receives a letter through the post informing him that his employment has been terminated. He is very angry. He had a heated discussion with one of the company directors last week about defects he had come across in the computer system, and he suspects the man has taken a dislike to him. He reckons that this is a case of wrong dismissal, and if the firm refuses to withdraw the redundancy notice he will complain to an Industrial Tribunal.

Doreen thinks positive

Doreen feels upset about losing her job. She was offered a job elsewhere within the group — but too far away for her to give it serious consideration. On the credit side the company have awarded her much more than the statutory minimum in redundancy pay and Doreen has gained a lot of useful experience and contacts which will help her embark on the next stage of her relaunched career. This is a time of new opportunity for her.

Edward: 'What about my pension?'

The axe has fallen at last on Edward's job. He is somewhat concerned about what will happen about his company pension and needs to discuss the matter with the pension administrator. He is also worried that at his age finding a new job could prove difficult. Nothing has yet been said about redundancy benefits or compensation so he needs to have a word with his immediate boss and the personnel department about the sort of redundancy package they envisage. He has made contact with a private careers counsellor and hopes the firm will be prepared to foot the bill.

1   Unemployment benefit in 1994 amounted to £45.45 per week.
2   Generally speaking, if your savings amount to more than £6,000 you will not be eligible. If your savings are between £3,000 and £6,000 you will receive a proportion of the total benefit. (Note: these figures are liable to change and should be checked.)
3   You can earn up to £2 a day without losing any benefit for that day. However if you exceed the lower earnings limit of £57 in a benefit week you could lose all your benefit (1994 amounts).

15
Changing Careers

Career progression can mean moving up the ranks of your organisation or moving on to a similar though better position with another employer (see Chapter 11). But there is a further option: turning your back on one career path and embarking on another.

A risky venture, you might feel. Yet today it is not uncommon to meet engineers who have become management consultants, teachers who have become financial advisers, scientists who have moved into public relations, army officers who have become bankers. While changing careers is not the easiest of options, you should certainly not reject the idea if the opportunity arises or circumstances permit.

There are two reasons for changing direction: because you *have* to and because you *want* to.

You *have* to change because

- prospects in your particular line of work are diminishing
- you can no longer perform your job satisfactorily (a problem with professional sportsmen among others).

You *want* to change because you feel

- you have reached a plateau and see no way of moving on
- the nature of your job has changed, reducing job satisfaction
- you learn of a better way of achieving your career objectives
- your career objectives have changed.

PREPARING FOR CHANGE

If you are young and in a fairly junior post changing direction can be relatively straightforward. For older people who have attained posts of responsibility in their original profession it is much more difficult, and may involve retraining and loss of salary. Certain options may be closed: for instance, it is a little too late for a 45 year old banker to train to be a brain surgeon.

The older you are, the greater the need for compromise. But even younger job changers need to realise that the chances are improved if you set your sights on a job sector which is expanding (*eg* tourism) rather than one that is in decline (*eg* coal mining).

Secondly, remember that success will come more readily if you start out with a clear idea of your aims and objectives. It is no use hoping that some job will turn up that appeals to you. You have to adopt a much more positive attitude and actively seek out new opportunities.

Thirdly, be fully aware of your aptitudes and abilities. If you are not, you may find it hard to convince a prospective employer that you are capable of making the jump to a different kind of job.

If you have any doubts, seek advice. Check your ideas — however undeveloped they may be — with a qualified careers counsellor and take note of any recommendations.

Seeking careers advice

If you are unsure of your next move you may need help to refocus your career strategy. This could come in the form of a consultation (or series of consultations) with a careers counsellor or a career development course.

If you decide to find help outside your organisation you could try:

The Employment Service (eg Job Centre)
This is really geared up to helping unemployed people get back into jobs. If you are made redundant you will meet a **New Client Adviser** when you register for unemployment benefit who will inform you of the free counselling facilities available to you. [1]

The local Careers Service
In the past this service concentrated on young people, but these days most services cater for adults as well. Advisers can offer advice on job opportunities within their area and point you in the direction of other sources of advice.

Colleges and universities
These institutions offer careers advice for their own students and may also run courses and a careers counselling service for outsiders.

Professional organisations and trade unions
A few of these offer a counselling service or career development courses for their members.

Employers
The armed services offer excellent facilities for servicemen and women who are returning to civvy street. Firms making employees redundant may offer redundancy counselling to affected staff (see Chapter 14).

Self-help groups
These are generally for people who are facing redundancy or who are currently jobless. Members meet regularly and share their experiences and may have access to professional counselling. Local libraries and Jobcentres may have details of those in your locality.

Independent careers counsellors
Some consultants offer a no frills service involving an assessment of your abilities, a one-off counselling session and perhaps a report in which possible career paths are suggested to you.

Others take you step by step through the stages of recruitment until you manage to find a job. Typically they offer a CV writing service, interview preparation and secretarial help.

Some even take much of the donkey work off your shoulders by marketing you (*ie* circulating your details to companies they feel could use your services). Such a service could be particularly attractive to people working in foreign countries where communications are poor who need someone on the spot to do their legwork for them. However, it does not normally come cheap.

A list of private careers counsellors appears in the Appendix.

Alternative forms of counselling
If you have faith in psychics, astrologers, graphologists, palmists and the like — there is no reason why you should not make use of their services. While they may not be able to direct you towards a specific career or job, they could well offer you the stimulus you need to start thinking out your next step towards permanent employment.

Selecting a careers counsellor
If you decide to engage the services of a careers counselling organisation, you should first ascertain:

- what services are being offered
- what qualifications and experience its counsellors have
- what their success rate is
- whether they subscribe to a code of ethics laid down by a professional organisation such as the British Association for Counselling.

If the fee is high you might also ask whether the firm in question offers you a written guarantee of 'money back if not successful'. You should also enquire how long it takes a client of theirs on average to find a job or effect a job change. Bear in mind that job search can be a lengthy process and that it is unrealistic to expect to achieve your goal in a couple of weeks.

It is possible — certainly in the case of a younger person — that you will be subjected to a battery of tests to determine your aptitude, personality and interests. This should lead to an **assessment** that indicates your strengths and latent abilities, and suggestions as to the career path (or paths) you should consider in order to make full use of these. However, the assessment and its recommendations should not be seen as the final word, but rather as the starting point for a discussion about the shape your career could take.

When you have completed your voyage of self-discovery, you may well feel sceptical, particularly if a change of direction is recommended. You need to discuss the feasibility of this recommendation. Are there actually openings for you in this particular discipline or sector, and if so, what are the prospects of your eventually landing a job? The advice offered by your counsellor needs to be relevant to your situation.

Knowing yourself

In Chapter 3 you were asked to assess yourself in terms of the skills you have to offer a prospective employer. Now you need to do the same thing, paying particular attention to your particular inclinations and interests which will give you some clues as to careers you might move into.

What kind of person are you now?

- Creative: are you an 'ideas' person? Do you have a strong imagination? Have you artistic flair?

- Open air: do you like to be out and about rather than stuck in an office?

- Practical: are you good at DIY? Do you like making things? Do you like to see results?

- Executive: do you like taking the lead? Are you a decision-maker?

- Gregarious: do you like meeting people? Do you get on well with others?

- Communicative: are you good with words? Are you able to put your ideas across?

- Numerate: are you good with figures?

- Scientific: are you more interested in processes than people?

- Systematic: are you a good organiser or planner?

- Philanthropic: are you keen to help and care for others?

- Analytical/intellectual: are you good at solving problems? Are you interested in ideas?

Here are ten occupations. Which of the above adjectives best describes each of them? In most cases more than one attribute is possible. Compare your answers with those on page 190.)

actuary, bursar, debt counsellor, designer, health service manager, laboratory technician, social worker, surveyor, theatre manager, tour guide.

IS A CHANGE FEASIBLE?

Having identified a vocation which looks promising, you need to consider how feasible it will be for you to change track. As already mentioned, change is usually easier for a person at the beginning of a career than for someone who is well into middle age and has a wide range of responsibilities. Yet, an increasing number of older people are opting for second careers these days.

If a change of career is likely to affect your nearest and dearest, make sure that you discuss the matter with them at length before you cast off into the unknown. Any step you take will have financial implications, so can you afford to make the change? Finally, you need to decide whether you are capable of making the transition from one kind of work to another.

Consider also that sacrifices may have to be made. You may be exchanging a well-paid job for a vocation which — particularly in the early stages — is far from lucrative and entails a degree of risk. You could well have to undergo a course of study or training which will make considerable demands on your intellectual resources and your pocket (see Chapter 12).

On the other hand, there are plenty of people who have moved successfully from one career path to another. The trend is, if anything, becoming more pronounced. You can benefit greatly by drawing on the experience of people who have successfully changed careers. Seek them out and ask them how they set about it, what snags they encountered, how they fared financially, what assistance they managed to obtain, and how long it took them to get established in their new career. A change of direction should not be a leap in the dark but a move that you set about in a methodical manner weighing up the pros and cons.

Even if you are a victim of circumstances (*eg* you have been made redundant or your contract has come to an end abruptly) adopt a calm, unhurried approach. Identify not one, but several different career paths you might consider, and see what opportunities present themselves.

Try to keep an open mind. Opportunities do not always have to be sought, but instead come out of the blue. The pity is that people sometimes fail to recognise them for what they are.

The best bets for a career changer

Other chapters in this book deal with opportunities abroad or as a self-employed person. If you prefer to be employed and based in the UK, you need to go for positions where you stand the best prospects of success.

Small businesses and organisations

Larger organisations tend to be hierarchical and inflexible, unable to accommodate late entrants into their career structure. In any case they are usually fully staffed. Small businesses, on the other hand, are less bureaucratic, often have greater growth prospects and offer greater scope for responsibility. However, do not expect a salary equivalent to that offered in a larger firm; smaller firms that are establishing themselves do not have that kind of money to spend.

Foreign firms that have recently arrived in your country
The development of a single unified European market means an influx
of firms — both from the Continent and the rest of the world —
wishing to set up offices and factories in the UK and Eire. In their
eyes a person with local knowledge (which they lack) could well be a
greater prize than someone with technical expertise (which they have
in abundance).

Sectors which are likely to undergo expansion
All predictions need to be taken with a pinch of salt. However, at
present the following sectors look particularly promising:

> Public relations
> Hi-tech industry
> Computer services
> Leisure industry
> Hotels and catering
> Education and training
> Voluntary bodies (charities)
> Management consultancy
> Services for the elderly
> Security

This list is by no means complete, and the situation could well
change over the next few years. Regular reading of the business press
should enable you to discern current trends.

Motherhood and career change
Many women face a radical change of lifestyle when they give birth
to children. Motherhood is itself a career and very much a full-time
job — particularly in the early stages of a child's development. If
children are to get off to a good start in life, they require a great deal
of care and attention that only a mother or father can provide.

In the past when families were large and life expectancy was shor-
ter it was regarded as normal for women to finish work when the first
child arrived in order to devote virtually the rest of their lives to
bringing up the family. However, times have changed and motherhood has ceased to be a lifelong career. Today's mother is likely to
spend less than half of her working life to bringing up a family, and
when the offspring have all grown up and left home the time can hang
heavy.

'If you leave your employment in order to bring up your children,'
so the argument goes, 'you will lose out in the promotion stakes;

which is why so few women become company directors.' An ambitious woman often feels torn between sacrificing her career outside the home for her family and sacrificing her family for her career outside the home.

Yet words like 'sacrifice' are an exaggeration. Motherhood needs to be viewed as a change of direction, albeit a temporary one. It will occupy much of your time for a decade or two, and there is no need to feel guilty about it. Later you will have the option of changing career again or returning to your original career.

In due course as your children grow older and spend time in school you may gradually re-establish links with the world of work outside the home by taking a part-time job or taking in fee-paying work. You may also find that motherhood creates spin-offs: you could, for instance, organise a job around your family by forming a play group or acting as an assistant in a nursery school.

Alternatively you could become a tele-worker: many people in what are considered high status professions — like authors! — work from home these days. A period of study during this time to update your skills or acquire new ones would be a useful investment for the future.

An alternative strategy — and one that has been followed in some areas of high male unemployment — is for the husband to stay at home and care for the children while the wife takes on the role of the breadwinner. And why not? Good career management allows you endless possibilities.

A job portfolio?

Instead of sticking to just one job, why not become a well paid two or three job person? There is currently a tremendous growth in the number of part-time jobs on offer as employers bring in more flexible employment policies. Retailing is one of the biggest employers of part-timers; education is another. Why not turn this trend to your advantage?

Another idea to consider is seasonal work. At certain times of the year many organisations need to take on extra staff for weeks or even months. The tourist industry, for example, employs many more people between April and October than at other times of the year; retailers need extra staff in the run-up to Christmas. One very good way of getting into this market is to contact an employment agency which specialises in temporary vacancies.

Having a job portfolio can be a liberating experience. With careful management you can build the jobs around your private life. If you work at weekends, you indulge in your passion for golf on weekdays when the links are less crowded. If you opt for jobs in the afternoon and evening, you could perhaps follow a course of study in the morning.

It is also excellent preparation if you are planning to become self-employed where you will need to juggle with a succession of assignments and clients (see Chapter 17).

CASE STUDIES

Angela looks for something new
Looking back on her first job Angela feels she ought try something completely different next time round. Indeed, it is quite usual for young people to try a number of different jobs before settling down, and changing direction is fairly easy at this stage. Angela would benefit from careers guidance to give her ideas on alternative careers she could tackle successfully, and should try the local authority careers office first of all.

Bob's need for direction
Bob is inwardly relieved that his first job has come to an end, but he dreads starting down another career path only to find he is not really suited to that either. He clearly needs to sort himself out, and a thorough career counselling session would be just the thing to enable him to discover the most fruitful career options.

Counselling for Colin
Colin has reached an age where he needs to review his career and plan for the future. Instead of looking for a job along the same lines as his last one, he should consider widening his experience by a change of direction or enrolling for further training as suggested in Chapter 12. Both suggestions would enhance his career prospects. A career counselling session would be a sensible investment as it would open Colin's eyes to opportunities which he has never considered.

Doreen begins to find her feet
Now that Doreen has found her feet again in the world of employment she has decided she would like to train for another profession. She is torn between social work and physiotherapy. Proper careers counselling would help to identify which of the two careers she is best suited for and perhaps turn up a few ideas that she has not considered.

Edward — could he pass on his knowledge?

Edward has no regrets that his job has folded, but he is unsure where
to go next, since he suspects most doors are closed to a person of his
age. He feels it is too late to train for a new career, but he could be
wrong. A session with a careers counsellor would help him to consider his situation and the various options that are open to him. Why
not pass on his knowledge and experience by becoming a technical
college lecturer, or go in for technical authorship? Or he could consider a portfolio of jobs, one of which could keep him fully occupied
well after retirement age.

[1]   See also the Department of Employment's booklet *Just the Job* obtainable from Jobcentres.

HOW TO MANAGE COMPUTERS AT WORK

Graham Jones

Assuming no prior knowledge, this is a really practical step-by-
step guide which puts the business needs of the user first. It
discusses why a computer may be needed, how to choose the
right one and instal it properly; how to process letters and documents, manage accounts, and handle customer and other records
and mailing lists. It also explains how to use computers for business presentations, and desktop publishing. If you feel you
should be using a computer at work, but are not sure how to
start, then this is definitely the book for you . . . and you won't
need an electronics degree to start!

'Bags of information in a lingo we can all understand. I
strongly recommend the book.' *Progress/NEBS Management
Association*. Graham Jones is Managing Director of a desktop
publishing company.

£8.99, 160pp illus. 1 85703 078 8
Please add postage & packing (UK £1 per copy.
Europe £2 per copy. World £3 per copy airmail).

How To Books Ltd,
Plymbridge House, Estover Road,
Plymouth PL6 7PZ, United Kingdom.
Tel: (0752) 695745. Fax: (0752) 695699. Telex: 45635.

Credit card orders may be faxed or phoned.

16
Venturing Overseas

Instead of changing career, how about opting for a change of climate? According to a survey conducted in 1993 nearly half the British population would like to go and live overseas, though only a small proportion actually do so.

When skies are leaden and job prospects at home look gloomy it is certainly tempting to consider a foreign assignment. However, working abroad should not be seen as a means of escape since you are unlike to find a posting which enables you to sit under palm tree on the beach sipping iced gin and tonic all day long.

Instead you have to be prepared to put in as much effort as you are doing in your present job — and more. You may be doing the same kind of work but in a different way. How you relate to your new surroundings could be just as crucial to your success as your professional expertise.

THE BENEFITS OF WORKING ABROAD

Viewed in the context of career development a spell overseas could be most beneficial. Young people who venture overseas often find that they are promoted to posts of responsibility much sooner than if they had remained at home. In some, but not all, circumstances attractive salaries are offered, but a more important consideration is that you are gaining really valuable international experience.

Working abroad has attractions for the older person as well. An overseas assignment could help pull you out of a rut and expose you to a range of new and stimulating challenges. You may be better equipped than a younger person to function in countries which are still decidedly low-tech in orientation and where the ability to handle people counts for more than IT expertise.

It could also launch you on an international career. Today national boundaries are losing their significance, notably within the European Union, and multinational firms and organisations are looking for people who can operate effectively in virtually any country of the world. Such ability can prove a valuable asset and should widen your choice of job opportunities.

FINDING A JOB

Unless you are exceptionally adventurous it makes sense to fix up your employment in advance. If you are already an employee, your first step should be to consult your employer and mention your willingness to be considered for overseas assignments. Although your own organisation may not do business abroad, it may have subsidiaries, affiliates or agents which do.

A second approach is to scour specialist publications for foreign job advertisements. These could be professional or trade magazines — such as the *Times Educational Supplement, Extraction News* and *Electronics Weekly* — or papers specialising in overseas job vacancies, such as *Nexus, Overseas Jobs Express*, and *Jobs International*. The quality newspapers also carry advertisements for jobs abroad.

You could also approach employers direct. Oil and construction companies, for instance, operate all over the world, and staff in their employment can expect a posting almost anywhere. If you become a member of the export sales department of most firms you can expect to be sent off on trips abroad and foreign postings might also be offered.

Do not overlook government organisations, such as the Diplomatic Service, the Overseas Development Administration, the British Council, the armed services and Crown Agents — or international organisations such as the United Nations and European Commission. People who feel that experience is worth more than a fat salary could work as a volunteer with VSO or a similar organisation, join an international charity, such as the Save the Children Fund, or become an overseas missionary.

Finally, there are plenty of private international recruitment agencies which often act as intermediaries for firms which do not have a base in the UK. Many of them specialise in certain sectors (*eg* health care, computers, engineering) and while some of the jobs they offer may be open-ended, most tend to be on a contract basis.

Most contracts are for between one and three years with perhaps the opportunity of an extension. It therefore makes sense to consider how you want your career to develop when the assignment is over. Some people build a career out of a succession of overseas contracts, but if it is your intention to rejoin the UK workforce eventually you need to plan your re-entry. If your contract is a fairly short one, try to fix up your next posting before you leave home.

If you see no vacancies in your field, make enquiries. Many professional institutions have international links and may well be able to point you in the right direction. You could, of course, visit a particular country on spec, but while this is easy enough in countries of the European Economic Area where there is free movement of labour, immigration authorities elsewhere require you to obtain a work permit before you travel.

Where and what the jobs are

Glance at one of the international jobs papers and you will discover that practitioners in certain skills, notably nursing, computing and electronics, are in demand all over the world. Teachers of English are needed to staff language schools in Europe and other non-English speaking countries; engineers and surveyors are needed for international construction projects. Accountants and lawyers with international experience are also much in demand.

The overseas jobs market is never static. At one time the Arabian Peninsula was regarded as an Eldorado for expatriates by virtue of the high salaries offered which were (and often still are) tax-free. While this area continues to be a major employer of expatriates there are also opportunities in the booming economies of the Far East. Eastern Europe is opening up to people with relevant expertise to transform economies into modern market-oriented ones.

Do not be disappointed if you find no advertisements for jobs in your favourite country. The most attractive countries are often the most difficult to find jobs in — either because of government restrictions on expatriate employment or because there is tremendous competition for what jobs exist. For these reasons you should not set your heart on a post in the Bahamas or Switzerland. In any case, the more attractive jobs could well be elsewhere.

YOUR FOREIGN POSTING

Some people take to living and working abroad like a duck to water, while others do not. If you have never worked in a foreign country before make sure that you are sufficiently adaptable and will be able to cope in a strange environment. Moving from Torquay to Timbuctoo does not merely represent a change of scene; you are entering a different culture where local attitudes and values may diverge fundamentally from your own.

Hence the importance of getting down to some research before you sign a contract or board a plane. Ideally your employer should provide you with a **briefing** either in-house or, even better, at a briefing centre. If nothing of the sort is offered, you should obtain a report on the place you are making for — from organisations such as Expat Network, Inside Tracks, Employment Conditions Abroad, Christians Abroad and Corona Worldwide. The latter three organisations can also arrange personal briefings.

Try, above all, to get some idea of the cost of living, since a salary of astronomical proportions is soon spent if food prices and rents are sky-high. A more modest honorarium accompanied by free accommodation could — in the long run — prove a much better bet.

For a single person or a young married couple with few commitments moving abroad presents very few problems. On the other hand, if you have a family, important decisions have to be made. Some posts will be **bachelor status** posts, which means you cannot take your family or spouse with you anyway, but you may have two or three leaves during the year to compensate for your lack of home life.

However, your position could involve a certain amount of entertaining, in which case the presence of your spouse could be important. This is fine in 'traditional' families where the husband is the main breadwinner, and the wife is prepared to follow him wherever he goes. But problems arise in 'dual career' families where the wife may not be so willing to interrupt her career and go off to organise cocktail parties in Port Moresby.

What of the children? Do you take them with you and hope that the local schools are adequate, or do you send them to boarding school or entrust them to a relative? While your life will be more complete if you follow the first option, your children's education could suffer if education provision at your posting is poor.

Examining the contract

If you take up employment overseas you will no longer be subject to UK labour laws. For this reason you should check your contract carefully particularly with respect to:

● Salary — is it net, tax free, or are there deductions? What currency will it be paid in? When and how frequently is it paid?

● Accommodation — is it provided free of charge, or must I pay rent? (If so, how much?) What does it consist of? Do I get a rent allowance?

- Working conditions — what precisely are my duties and working hours? Who am I responsible to?

- Visas and work permits — who is responsible for getting these and what is the procedure?

- Health provision — am I insured against illness? What kind of medical treatment can I expect? What provision is there for sick leave?

- Provision for my dependents — is it an accompanied or bachelor status post? If the former, are there extra allowances for family and educational provision for my children?

- Pension provision — what are the pension arrangements, if any? Or is a gratuity payable instead of a pension?

- Length of contract — is it open ended or fixed term (with the possibility of renewal)? When does it come into effect?

- Perks — if there are any, what form do they take? (*eg* free transport, bonuses, free medical care, duty free import privileges).

- Tax — what is my tax liability — abroad and in the UK?

- Termination of contract — what provision is there for the premature termination of the contract? What is the procedure in the event of a dispute?

Will a foreign lifestyle suit you?

Will you be able to make a go of things in a foreign environment? Not every overseas posting proves a success. Some people have such difficulty in adjusting to their new environment that they have to be repatriated; others perform less effectively than at home.

Even if you are only crossing the Channel to work you will have to come to grips with different customs and a different language. If you are heading for Central Africa you will also have a different climate to contend with as well as a different attitude towards work.

You may find that you have to change your style completely since the very attributes which worked to your advantage at home may be quite out of place in an alien culture. A tough, no-nonsense approach may be considered rudeness in Asia, and hard drinking will alienate you from strict Muslim society.

Adaptability and good health are both essential. If you have spent some of your formative years in foreign parts, you will have an inkling of what to expect. But if like Noel Coward's Uncle Harry you set off for a distant land with poor preparation, you could be in for a shock.

For some it can be much worse, particularly if their personal affairs are in a fragile state even before they arrive at their post. Resorting to booze and drugs will not help to remedy problems. They will only serve to accentuate them in an environment where appropriate help is not often available.

Good communication skills — both verbal and non-verbal — are a must. In a good many countries you will need to speak the language of the locals. You may find yourself a member of a multi-national team where the scope for misunderstandings is compounded and patience and understanding are at a premium.

Assessing your suitability

Before you commit yourself to working abroad, assess your suitability for a foreign posting — that of any accompanying dependents too. Look at the following features and try to rate yourself on a five point scale (1 low — 5 high) and compare your answers with the comments on page 191.

Personal feature	*Rating*
Adaptability	_____
Health	_____
Language and communication skills	_____
Resourcefulness	_____
Stability	_____
Qualifications	_____
Experience abroad	_____
Patience	_____
Tact	_____
Respect for other cultures	_____

Expertise alone is not enough

If this chapter has dwelt excessively on the pitfalls of working abroad, the aim is certainly not to discourage the many people who embark on challenging tasks overseas every year and find their feet straight away. Some are so exhilarated by the experience that they become career expatriates.

Yet competence and expertise in your chosen field are not sufficient in themselves; personal attitudes and skills are just as essential to the success of an overseas posting. If you are deficient in courtesy, patience, understanding of others, flexibility and resilience, this could prove a disastrous option — for your employer, your family, yourself and your career.

CASE STUDIES

A 'gap year' for Angela?

A spell abroad could be an excellent idea, but it should not be too long. If she decides to go on to higher education Angela could defer the start of her course for a year and spend time working in a foreign country — perhaps as an au pair — in order to broaden her experience and improve her language skills. There are a number of publications which suggest opportunities for the so-called gap year. The main drawback is that many of these opportunities are on a volunteer basis or do not pay particularly well.

Bob needs to decide his priorities

A job abroad could prove a sensible idea and offer valuable experience, especially if it forms part of a well-thought out career plan. Bob has seen one or two contract posts that appeal to him, but he is rather unsure how he will cope when the contract comes to an end. Sooner or later he needs to get his foot on the career ladder and if his real objective is to make his career in the UK, he should be trying to gain experience here first of all.

A new horizon for Colin?

This could be an excellent plan for Colin. He would be adding an international dimension to the experience he has accumulated, making him an attractive proposition to future employers. Moreover he should be able to command a renumeration package well in excess of his current earnings which would enable him to save money for a time when family responsibilities will prove a heavy financial burden.

Doreen puts family first

What? Abandon her husband and children to take up a posting in some distant land? For the time being Doreen needs to stay put — unless her husband manages to get an overseas posting where she can accompany him. In five or ten years' time when she is free of all her domestic responsibilities it might be a completely different matter.

A new life for Edward?

This is an option well worth considering, since he is more mobile than he has been for years. Finding an overseas post might even be easier than finding one in the UK where Edward may encounter age discrimination; other countries, by contrast, are more appreciative of mature, experienced people. If his first contract proves a success there may be a possibility of a succession of further contracts which will keep him busy until he decides to retire.

17
Doing Your Own Thing

'Why work to make other people rich? Why not work for yourself instead?'

The idea of becoming your own boss sounds very attractive. People dream of owning a country pub or setting up an engineering workshop, and recall how some of the greatest firms in the land started from very modest roots.

These days entrepreneurship is encouraged, and there is plenty of support and advice available for potential entrepreneurs. However, before you blow all your savings on a pet scheme which, if unsuccessful, might leave you penniless, it is wise to weigh up the pros and cons.

Setting up on your own can be a risky business — especially if you have no previous experience of self-employment — so you must ensure that you have the skills, qualities and resources that will ensure success. Enthusiasm and a good idea is not enough. It is a sobering thought that — according to one source — four fifths of all businesses fail during their first five years.

GETTING ADVICE

No explorer would consider setting out on an expedition without maps, proper equipment and a survival manual, but it is surprising how many people set up their own businesses with only a hazy appreciation of what this step entails.

Yet — certainly as far as the UK is concerned — advice is readily and usually freely available from bodies like **local enterprise boards** and **Training and Enterprise Councils**. Sources such as these not only produce useful booklets for people starting their own businesses, but may also offer free counselling sessions at which your plans are discussed and analysed by experienced people.

If the counsellor makes encouraging noises, you can plan your next move. If you are a trifle daunted by talk of cash flow projections and liquidity ratios, you should either get yourself a good accountant or enlist for a **Training for Enterprise** course. There are also open learning schemes provided by organisations like the Open College and the Industrial Society which should help you carry out a feasibility study on your enterprise and take you through the elements of running a business step by step.

There is no catch in all these schemes. Many local authorities as well as the government are keen to encourage new businesses since you are not only creating an opportunity for yourself, but as time goes on you could also be creating employment for others.

A session with your bank manager would not be inappropriate at this stage in the proceedings. In due course you will need to open a separate account for your business, discuss the terms of the account, and perhaps apply for a loan. Normally bankers play safe when it comes to lending money to businesses with no track record, but if in Britain you mention the government's **Loan Guarantee Scheme** your bank manager should become more amenable.

You do not, of course, need to use your own bank, and it pays to shop around to find one which is especially keen on helping small businesses and keeps bank charges low. Some publish booklets expressly designed for people who are setting up their own businesses.

PAYING ATTENTION TO CASH FLOW

One matter which may deter you from launching out on your own is that you may not derive any income from the business until it has been built up. Indeed you may face a loss for the first year. You must also cope with the fact that payments are often delayed while bills have to be settled promptly. If you fail to keep a tight rein on your finances, you could experience a cash flow crisis (*ie* not enough money to pay your bills although you are due to be paid eventually).

Rather than start off with ambitious plans which require considerable investment the best policy is normally to play safe. Start off in a small way, re-invest your profits and build up the business slowly but safely.

Of course, this may not always be possible. If you have a new invention you wish to exploit, a large capital outlay may be needed to get it into production. In the end you might decide to have the product manufactured under licence. Possible financial hardship is mitigated (though hardly alleviated) in the UK by the government's **Business Start Up Programme**. [1]

Many a small business starts off as a part-time occupation supplementing a person's regular earnings. Yet even when the enterprise starts to occupy the bulk of your time it is often prudent to have an alternative source of income to keep you afloat at times when business is poor. If you set up an ice cream business, for instance, you will find that trade falls off as the temperature goes down; you might well be glad to have an undemanding part-time job to fall back on in the depths of winter.

It is instructive to read the autobiographies of entrepreneurs, just to find how they coped in the early days before they became household names. Indeed you will learn a deal about the pitfalls of running a business just by reading books and by looking around you to see which businesses are flourishing and which are not. Analysing the problem of a badly run enterprise can be just as illuminating as looking at a really efficient outfit.

WHAT SKILLS DO YOU NEED?

Look at the following attributes. How do you score? The maximum mark for each attribute is 5.

Business skill	Rating
Marketing skills	_____
Financial acumen	_____
Capital available	_____
Technical expertise	_____
Organisational skills	_____
Health	_____
Initiative	_____
Persistence	_____
Motivation	_____
Self-confidence	_____

For answers and comments see the Appendix.

PARTNERS AND FRANCHISES

A sensible business owner will always seek to minimise risk and maximise profit,though sad to say caution is sometimes abandoned.

You can diminish risk by going in with a partner, preferably one who possesses skills in which you are deficient and whom you know to be trustworthy and reliable.

A battle-scarred business veteran can be a formidable partner, and may well infuriate you with what seems a negative attitude towards your grandiose plans. If the operation is not to go under, commercial considerations sometimes have to outweigh all others. However, you need to choose your partner with great care, since many partnerships eventually turn sour.

Franchising

Another way of spreading the risk is to link up with a franchisor. Business format franchising began in the USA in the 1950s and subsequently spread to Britain and other countries. The idea is that you are supplied with the franchisor's knowhow in return for a fee and/or a percentage of the profits.

A number of establishments in your high street, such as Mc-Donald's, Kentucky Fried Chicken, Tie Rack and Body Shop, are operated by local people under licence. There are some 300 different franchise systems in Britain alone and they include employment bureaux, estate agencies, insurance brokers, car engine tuning businesses, print shops and cleaning services. Annual sales in franchised outlets are around £5 billion, so they are clearly a force to be reckoned with.

A possible drawback with franchise operations is you are not in complete control of your own business, since you are expected to conform to certain standards. In the event of any disagreement the franchise can be terminated. On the other hand, if you are sheltering under the umbrella of a famous name which has a well-tried formula, the chances of success are fairly bright. According to the British Franchise Association the current failure rate is a mere 3.8%.

Before becoming too involved you would be advised to take independent financial and legal advice, to ensure that the deal does not turn out to be biased in favour of the franchisor. You should also talk at length to other franchisees of the firm you are interested in collaborating with and find out the snags before you commit yourself irrevocably. If the franchisor is unwilling to let you do this, make sure he has a really convincing explanation.

The British Franchise Association — an organisation which exists to promote the concept of franchising — can supply details of how a franchise works and a list of its members. There are a number of books on the subject of franchising and consultants who specialise in this field.

WHAT TYPE OF BUSINESS?

In many cases would-be entrepreneurs have a clear idea of the kind of business they wish to set up. Others do not, or else they are not aware of the variety of options open to them. You can:

Use the skills you already have
An accountant or a lawyer starts his own practice; a teacher opens his own school or tutorial business; a designer sets up his own design shop; a parent starts up a day nursery.

Build on your spare time skills and interests
People often overlook the fact that over the years they have developed expertise in their leisure pursuits as well as in their professional work. So consider whether you have any hobbies which could become your full-time occupation (*eg* a tennis coach, a professional model maker, an artist).

Enter a completely new field
Such a course is not without its pitfalls. Running a restaurant or a small shop is not as easy is it looks, and you need to have some idea of the tricks of the trade before you set out. However, if you are versatile and have good business skills, there is no reason why you should not be successful provided you prepare carefully for the challenge.

POINTERS TO SUCCESS

There is no sure-fire recipe for success in business. If you opt for self-employment, you will, of course, need to put in a lot of hard work. Even then, if this hard work is misdirected, the business could run into trouble. You could also find yourself in the wrong place at the wrong time — a victim of economic recession or changing taste.

Some key guidelines
There are however a few guidelines which no newly fledged entrepreneur should ignore. While they do not guarantee success, they should at least lessen the possibility of failure.

Do your homework before you take the plunge
Firstly, ensure that there is a market for your product or service. Then work out how much time and money you will need to invest before you get a return. In other words, work out a business plan.

Start off with sufficient capital
Most new small businesses are undercapitalised, which means that they have no resources to see them through lean times. You need to have sufficient cash to see you through at least the first year of trading.

Promote yourself effectively
Many businesses start off as a good idea, but fail because of inadequate promotion. Rather than shy away from publicity, you must be an out-and-out self-publicist — particularly in the early days of your project — spending a significant proportion of your time out and about making contacts.

Take a long-term view
It usually takes time to build up a sound business, and you may not start to reap the fruits of your endeavours until your second or third year.

Learn to manage your time efficiently
If you are self-employed, you need to use every minute to fullest effect. Set yourself priorities and learn to work to a strict routine.

Do not count on getting a regular income — especially in the early stages
It is in the nature of certain businesses for payments to arrive in fits and starts. Indeed, it is only the bills that come in with monotonous regularity. You have to accept that in some months expenditure is likely to exceed income and be prepared for the shortfall.

The customer is king
Every client, no matter how significant, has the power to make or break you. If satisfied with the service, they will recommend you to others. If not, they are likely to pass on adverse impressions and so deter others from doing business with you. You must therefore accord every client the highest priority.

Business considerations must always come first
You will have to exercise strict financial control and plan ahead. This may well mean that you have to cut down on some of the more interesting parts of your work in order to concentrate on less exciting matters such as book-keeping, business forecasts and marketing.

Recognise that you are the person in the driving seat
You have to make the decisions and take responsibility for them. At

times these may be very hard decisions, which you feel ill-equipped to deal with, but eventually you will manage to take them in your stride.

Is self-employment worth the trouble?

Setting up your own business, while not quite in the same league as the labours of Hercules, can come pretty close to it. Yet there are plenty of successful self-employed individuals in every country — from accountants to farmers, plumbers to solicitors — and many of them will have faced similar problems to those you will encounter, particularly in the early stages.

A fluctuating income can be alarming to anyone who has been used to a monthly salary cheque. It is just as perturbing to recognise that —for the first time in your life, perhaps — the success or failure of your enterprise depends entirely on your own efforts.

On the other hand 'your own thing' can be an exhilarating experience despite a bank overdraft. Furthermore, your mental and physical health will be better than that of the average employee. You could come to relish your independence knowing that in a flourishing business you are the person who takes the credit — and the cash — for its success, not someone else further up the line.

CASE STUDIES

Angela needs more experience

Although some entrepreneurs start businesses while in their teens (*eg* Richard Branson, Alan Sugar of Amstrad), they are very much the exception. Angela has much to learn about the world of work and the best place to do this is in a structured work environment as an employee. Going alone might be an option once she has gained experience and grown in self-confidence.

Bob's need for experience

Bob would be better advised to find employment initially, since he needs to find out how the workplace operates. It is easier at some later stage to move from employment to self-employment than vice versa.

Colin — enough energy and capital?

Colin is still in his first flush of youth — relatively speaking — and has plenty of energy to devote to setting up his own business if he is so minded. However, he needs to have plenty of capital behind him and be prepared to operate at a loss for the first year or so. Since he already has heavy financial commitments it might be wise to put this off for a few years. Alternatively he might consider a franchise operation since partnerships of this nature are less likely to fail and banks are generally more willing to offer loans to franchise holders.

Doreen — an interesting possibility

This could be a sensible option for Doreen, and a number of returners have taken this path. She could, for instance, operate as a freelance secretary handling correspondence and other documentation for small businessmen. If she has sufficient capital she could open a shop. However, she needs to develop more self-confidence, perhaps by taking a self-assertiveness course at the local college of further education.

Edward's dilemma

Edward has plenty of experience behind him and a reasonable amount of capital. While he may not be young enough to build up a business empire in the years ahead, he could probably set up a profitable business — perhaps with his wife as a partner — an antique shop, perhaps, or a specialist garden furniture business. Self-employment, however, is not an option for the faint-hearted, and he will need to expend considerable effort to get his venture off the ground. The local enterprise agency will be able to furnish him with the necessary advice on how to proceed.

[1] In 1994 the Enterprise Allowance in the UK amounted to £40 per week and was payable for 6 months.

18
Looking Ahead

What is the extent of your 'time horizon'?[1] How far can you see ahead? If you possess tremendous vision you may be able to see 50 years ahead; many people, however, can only see a few months ahead; some only a day or so into the future. Yet career management is a long term project, requiring forward planning and long term goals. Ideally we need to understand the state of society and the jobs market in the year 2040.

Why the year 2040? Because this is the year when young people who are now starting work will be reaching the climax of their careers — and yet nobody can be certain what they will be doing then. Who would have predicted the rise of the computer programmer or digital telecommunications engineer 45 years ago when the technology simply did not exist?

After 150 years steam trains have now run their course; they are now museum pieces. In offices typewriters and duplicators have been superceded by word processors and photocopiers within little more than a decade. Might not the motor car and the all-pervasive computer experience a similar fate?

In fact, it is reasonable to suppose that many familiar aspects of our life will become obsolete early in the next century and this will have implications for all of us. The trouble is we cannot tell which ones they will be — unless we have exceptional vision.

TOWARDS THE YEAR 2000

Even between now and the end of the decade structural changes are taking place in the employment markets. Demographic trends mean that far fewer school and college leavers will join the workforce over the next few years. A large proportion of the shortfall will be accounted for by women workers returning to work.

There will also be sectoral changes. 'The main areas of employment growth over the medium term are . . . expected to be amongst managerial, professional and associate professional jobs. In contrast the number of jobs for craft and skilled manual workers, plant and machine operatives, and unskilled labourers is expected to fall substantially.'[2] Those manual workers who remain will need to develop higher levels of skill.

These findings are borne out by McKinsey (Amsterdam). They predict that by the end of this century 70% of all jobs in Europe will require cerebral rather than manual skills — the complete reverse of the situation in 1900. Half of these will need higher education or a professional qualification. This trend augurs well for women: these are jobs which do not require physical strength so they can compete successfully with men.

Another estimate suggests that by the year 2000 12 million people will be in full-time jobs, while 12 million will be self-employed, part-time or temporary workers. More firms will become 'shamrock' organisations, according to Professor Charles Handy, consisting of a core of essential executives and workers supported by outside contractors and part-time help.[3] Increasingly temporary executives and consultants will be engaged to turn round companies or departments.

Information of this nature is vital for managers — and especially for you as you start to manage your career. If you can detect the underlying trends, you will be in a good position to take decisive action — to retrain, to rethink your career strategy, to move into a more promising job sector. If you fail to act, you face a bleak outlook of diminishing job prospects and even unemployability.

CHANGING OUR IDEAS

One danger we must avoid is to let our thinking be trapped in a time warp, and assume that the future will be a continuation of the present only much improved. With current developments the future may bear little relation to what has gone before. 'Discontinuous change requires discontinuous thinking,' writes Professor Charles Handy.[3]

We therefore need to reexamine several concepts that we have tended to take for granted such as the ones listed below.

the 5 day week	casual and part-time jobs
a career for life	retraining
one job per person	working in offices and factories
promotion ladders	company loyalty
retirement age	self-employment

Are these concepts likely to remain the norm well into the next century? — or will we have to accept radically different approaches? Compare your ideas with those suggested in the Appendix.

Accepting new career patterns

For the last hundred years people's lives have broadly followed three stages. First, people went to school and perhaps college, then found a job, and finally continued working until reaching retirement age. We can show this in a diagram form:

This was fine while it lasted but as we approach the end of the millennium we have to face up to new realities. For instance, your initial education is unlikely to see you through to the end of your career. Older people may complain about 'ageism' in company recruitment policies, and women returners about 'discrimination'. In reality it is not so much their age or sex which is at issue, it is the fact that they are not up-to-date.

As you get to grips with managing your career it would help if you could view the way ahead not as a straight path leading ever upwards but as a continuing cycle as shown below.

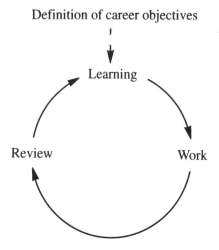

Sometimes the learning will be concurrent with the work — continuing professional development in the form of in-service training, evening classes or other forms of part-time training. At other times you may need a longer period of more intensive study and training in order to prepare for greater responsibilities or change career direction entirely.

If you look around you will find that this pattern is being adopted by more and more people, all the time.

Planning your career timetable

Perhaps the time has come to view our efforts in a different light. The boundaries between work and retirement, work and study, work and leisure, work and home life are becoming blurred.

Professor Charles Handy[3] identifies five kinds of work:

- Wage work: employment where we are paid for the *time* given.
- Fee work: work we do for clients where we are normally paid for *results*.
- Home work: household tasks, gardening, bringing up a family, etc.
- Gift work: voluntary work, public service.
- Study.

The first two kinds of work are those for which we are paid. The final three are unpaid — yet they require real effort and are hardly a form of relaxation. At any stage of our lives we are all involved in one of these activities; many of us might be involved in a mix of two or three at one time. Moreover the pattern can change considerably over the course of your career.

Figure 12 illustrates the kind of pattern that some people already have. The beginning of the career is marked by intensive study with perhaps some part-time employment (a vacation job?), some voluntary work along with various household chores. Then several years of full-time paid employment and expanding household chores with the acquisition of a house and garden and perhaps marriage and children. Sometime around this stage the second example finds that most of her activity comes into the 'work at home' category.

Two periods of study are programmed, perhaps in anticipation of promotion, a job change or a career change. From the age of forty onwards the person in the first example takes a keen interest in civic affairs and becomes a councillor. In his fifties he decides to start a small business in his spare time. The business later expands to

How will you spend your working life?

Age (years)	Study (%)	Wage work (%)	Fee work (%)	Homework (%)	Gift work (%)
Male					
20	70 _____	10 _____	0 _____	10 _____	10 _____
25	0 _____	80 _____	0 _____	0 _____	10 _____
30	0 _____	80 _____	0 _____	20 _____	0 _____
35	40 _____	40 _____	0 _____	10 _____	10 _____
40	0 _____	80 _____	10 _____	10 _____	10 _____
45	0 _____	75 _____	0 _____	10 _____	15 _____
50	5 _____	70 _____	5 _____	10 _____	10 _____
55	0 _____	60 _____	20 _____	10 _____	10 _____
60	0 _____	0 _____	70 _____	10 _____	20 _____
65	5 _____	0 _____	65 _____	15 _____	15 _____
70	10 _____	0 _____	30 _____	30 _____	30 _____
75	5 _____	0 _____	20 _____	50 _____	25 _____
Female					
20	70 _____	10 _____	0 _____	10 _____	10 _____
25	0 _____	90 _____	0 _____	10 _____	0 _____
30	5 _____	0 _____	0 _____	85 _____	10 _____
35	5 _____	0 _____	0 _____	85 _____	10 _____
40	10 _____	25 _____	0 _____	65 _____	0 _____
45	5 _____	50 _____	0 _____	45 _____	0 _____
50	0 _____	60 _____	0 _____	30 _____	10 _____
55	0 _____	40 _____	20 _____	30 _____	10 _____
60	0 _____	30 _____	30 _____	30 _____	10 _____
65	5 _____	0 _____	30 _____	60 _____	5 _____
70	0 _____	0 _____	20 _____	60 _____	20 _____
75	0 _____	0 _____	0 _____	70 _____	30 _____

Fig. 12. The changing pattern of work. Although individual circumstances may differ greatly, here are some typical examples of how we are likely to spend our time in future. What about your own working life? In the spaces provided, you can write the percentages of your own time you have spent on each activity, so far, and the time you expect to spend on each in the future. For definitions of headings, see text.

become a full-time occupation, which continues — albeit at a lower level — after the official age of retirement.

It must be stressed that these are just examples of the pattern that your career might take — not models to be followed scrupulously.

Note that two words do not appear on the diagram: unemployment and retirement. If you are managing your career properly you should not have periods of enforced idleness; if these threaten you either change jobs or career direction or you arrange for a sabbatical.

Retirement has been left out because it is a misleading word implying that you stop work when you reach the age of 65 or so. Most people do not, though the nature of their work may change.

MOVING INTO THE THIRD AGE

One of the greatest shocks a person can experience is to be in a job one day and out of work the next. You suddenly feel disoriented; you have lost your status as an employee and perhaps also your purpose in life. This can happen when you are suddenly made redundant or when you retire.

If you have been managing your career successfully you will not be caught unawares when the axe falls on your job. You will be ready to deal with the situation. But retirement is a different matter; like death it seems inevitable.

Enforced retirement is especially traumatic if you have achieved a senior position in your organisation and you enjoy your work. To be reduced to pottering about the house after a life full of activity can be hard to take, and you may suffer depression and other ills as a consequence. But this kind of come-down can be avoided.

In 1990 the Carnegie UK Trust undertook an inquiry into the so-called third age.[4] Initially this was seen as 'the period after full-time work ended'. However, as its work went on the Inquiry redefined it as 'a period of increasing freedom from the structures of work and of a family with dependent children preceding what for some is a period of increasing disablement and dependency which we have termed the "fourth age" '. The third age now refers to the 50-75 age group.

This new definition reflects changed realities. Since 1901 life expectancy at birth has increased from 45 to 73 for men and from 49 to 79 for women. Today a fifty year old man can live to 75; a fifty year old woman to 81. There are not only many more people over the age of 50, but they tend to be fitter and more active than their predecessors. Today 12% of 65-69 year olds have full-time jobs and 72% work part-time.

Many people will live well beyond 75; indeed by the year 2031 9% of the UK population will be above this age. The majority will enjoy good health thanks to improved medical care and the elimination of some killer diseases, and healthy people need a purpose in life. They also need a reasonable income, yet there is some doubt as to whether governments will be able to afford generous state handouts to an ever-increasing band of pensioners.

For these reasons as you grow older, the need to manage your future really increases rather than diminishes. Retirement does not need to be a case of 'job today, none tomorrow'; it can be phased in. So when you attain the age of 50 you ought to sit back and plan ahead for your next 30, 40 or even 50 years. Since your career horizon will have grown with your increasing maturity, you should find this less difficult than earlier in your life.

Bear in mind that far from nearing the end of your career, you are embarking on a new phase of your life, free to embark on tasks offering greater fulfilment. Retiring from the world about you is unlikely to offer such fulfilment, and you should seriously consider ways in which you could extend your career.

For instance:

● you might explore the self-employment option

● you might develop a portfolio of part-time jobs which can be reduced as time goes by

● you might increase the time devoted to unpaid activities, or

● you could strike out in a new career direction.

All of these ideas will keep you active well after the official retirement age so you will not suffer sudden loss of status. Having a career into retirement will keep you healthy and happy.

This might also be a good time to consider retraining, so that you keep fully in touch with contemporary developments. But you need to act promptly and decisively or else you could find it hard to achieve your goal.

CASE STUDIES

Angela in 2040?
Angela's career is likely to stretch beyond the year 2040 and it is very hard to tell what she will be doing then. The jobs that some of her

contemporaries are interested in (*eg* secretarial work, routine clerical work) may well be extinct — computers or robots having taken over much of the routine office work. She will have to be prepared to go to college . . . again and again and again.

Bob in 2030?
Bob will be in his prime in the year 2030 and possibly on his fifth or sixth job at least. His job title will be utterly meaningless to us now because nothing like it exists at present. Bob has decided that he must have a sabbatical every ten years even if he has to finance it himself, and this bodes well for a very successful career.

Colin in 2020?
Colin needs to plan ahead for the next 25 years at least and should try to work out what his next four jobs are going to be. He also needs to improve his qualifications during the next few years as he is likely to face tough competition from well educated youngsters and women returners who have upgraded their knowledge and may know more than he does. Colin also ought to broaden his range of interests. Working out a timetable for the rest of his career is a priority.

Doreen in 2020?
After a decade during which her career has been dominated by home work Doreen has at least 25 years of a career before her. That is why it is worth taking steps to prepare for it rather than take a job or succession of jobs which do not allow her to make full use of her talents. Somehow she will have to juggle housework, a part-time job and a part-time course — perhaps with the Open University, which requires very careful time management, but in the end it should be worth it.

Edward in 2010?
Edward should also be looking ahead. He may be thinking about retirement in 10 or 15 years from now but he may have different views as the fateful day approaches. The chances are that he will be in excellent health and will want to lead quite an active life, in which case he needs to take steps to develop interests that will take him beyond the age of retirement. His fee paying and non paying work will become more important in his life.

AND FINALLY

This books ends as it began with a look into the future, which you may feel poses more questions than it answers. But the right question can often be more fruitful than the wrong solution, especially if it prompts you to search for the right answer.

If you are young, like Angela and Bob, most of your career will unfold in the next century where new ideas and new methods will come into play. 'You can never plan the future by the past,' writes Edmund Burke, [5] and for this reason you should not rely completely on what has been established practice for the last fifty years.

Managing your career in the workplace of tomorrow may well call for different skills along the lines suggested by Rosabeth Moss Kanter:

- A belief in self rather than in the power of position alone.

- The ability to collaborate and become connected with new teams in various ways.

- Commitment to the intrinsic excitement of achievement in a particular project than can show results.

- The willingness to keep learning.[6]

Even if your time horizon is limited, you can compensate by reviewing your career on a regular basis, just as an experienced investor reviews his share portfolio, and then taking appropriate action. As a manager you should not shun the challenge of the future however uncertain it may be. 'The age of unreason is an age of opportunity even if it looks at first sight more like the end of all ages.' [3]

---

[1] 'Time horizon is the longest period into the future within which a person is capable of organising and carrying through given tasks or projects, handling problems as they arise on the way, and reaching the goal.' Elliott Jacques, *Executive Leadership*, Blackwell 1991.

[2] *Review of the Economy and Employment*, Institute for Employment Research 1992.

[3] *The Age of Unreason*, Charles Handy (Business Books 1989).

[4] *Life, Work and Livelihood in the Third Age: Final Report*, Carnegie UK Trust 1993.

[5] *Letter to a Member of the National Assembly*, Edmund Burke.

[6] *When Giants Learn to Dance*, Rosabeth Moss Kanter (Routledge 1992).

Appendix: Solutions and Comments

CHAPTER 1

Trades and professions

Bank clerk
Already automation is taking over as banks try to contain costs. Cash machines are now being introduced that can process a wide range of transactions. Job likely to disappear.

Car mechanic
The car is likely to become as obsolete as the horse and buggy. Even if it stays around improved technology means that it will not require repairs. Job likely to disappear.

Doctor
Doctors will probably be around but their job will have changed. Computers will diagnose what is wrong with you and surgeons will merely programme computers to perform operations thus eliminating human error. Job will be unrecognisable.

Pilot
The technology already exists to fly unmanned aeroplanes. If model aircraft can be radio controlled, surely their larger brethren can be. Job likely to disappear except at displays of vintage aircraft such as the Airbus or Concorde.

Politicians
This is one of the oldest professions on earth and is unlikely to disappear.

Printer
News is now available on TV and books are available on database

and CD ROM (Computer Disc Read Only Memory). The technology is available to enable us to do away with printed matter altogether. No more trees cut down for paper. No more printers.

Secretary/typist
The technology is now available to enable spoken words to be reproduced in written form, which can then be transmitted to the workstation of the recipient. Secretaries may well become obsolete.

Social worker
This is a person to person profession, and is still likely to be around, though the techniques used will change.

Teacher
Pupils will be so adept at handling computerised learning programmes that classroom teaching as we know it will have disappeared. The teacher is likely to become a learning manager who decides which interactive programmes to use.

Train driver
The Docklands Railway in London has driverless trains and this concept could eventually extend to the whole railway network — if we are still using trains then. Train drivers are likely to become a thing of the past — like coachmen.

Comment
You may not agree with all the predictions but they should give you food for thought.

CHAPTER 2

The Henley Forecasting Centre published the following survey of attitudes to work in 1988.

Having control over what you do	50% of respondents
Using knowledge and experience to make decisions	50%
Having a variety of things to do	39%
Amount you earn	35%
Being with and making friends	21%
Doing a job you know people respect	19%

CHAPTER 3

The skills were ranked in the following order of importance by Lucas:

1 analytical skills
2 flexibility
3 decision making skills
4 ability to make independent judgements
5 numeracy
6 adaptability
7 intra-personal skills
8 communication skills
9 ability to work as a team
10 problem solving skills

CHAPTER 4

Choosing an employment agency

Anders Glaser Wills: recruit engineers, mainly for overseas.

Astron: specialises in publishing.

James Baker: specialises in senior IT people for positions at home and abroad.

BNA: British Nursing Association. Recruits nursing staff for establishments both at home and abroad.

Gabbitas Truman & Thring (now Gabbitas Educational Services): recruits teachers for private schools at home and abroad.

Harrison Willis: specialises in accountancy recruitment.

Jobcentre: this arm of the Government's Employment Service recruits for all kinds of jobs, including temporary and secretarial work though not normally executive posts. Also recruits for abroad.

Quarry Dougall: legal positions, including overseas jobs.

Travail: recruits for a wide range of jobs both temporary and permanent.

Universal Aunts: recruits for domestic work including gardeners, au pairs, companions, cooks.

VIP Recruitment: specialises in hotel and catering positions at home and abroad.

CHAPTER 5

Comparing application letters

The first letter is just a covering letter and not very inspiring. Let us hope that the accompanying CV has more impact.

The second letter is slightly better than the first in that it gives brief details of the candidate. but there is nothing in the letter which makes you want to read on. Foresters and lawyers are two a penny, and a selector will need some persuasive evidence that Mr Hood can do the job.

The third letter has a good deal more sparkle and tries to relate the candidate's skills to the job. It also sounds very positive thanks to words like *successfully, improved, increased, established, innovatory, responsible, motivation.* Provided the CV is as good as the letter this Mr Hood stands a good chance of making it to the shortlist.

CHAPTER 6

Choosing the appropriate CV type

CV Model 1 is the standard type of CV that a school or college leaver might produce. It includes a good deal of useful information, but could benefit from a little more detail.

Model 2 is very interesting. Mr Hood describes his achievements and uses positive vocabulary.

Model 3 is a humorous alternative CV, which by its very form conveys a good idea of the kind of person Mr Carruthers is. It might amuse and even stimulate the curiosity of a jaded selector, though a person without a sense of humour might discard it right away. A risky document, but then any manager worth his salt must be prepared to take risks.

Model 4 is a cunning way of presenting a good deal of information in a digestible manner and within a small amount of space. It is a format that some recruitment agents use when presenting candidates to clients. If you have a long and varied career behind you it might be worth considering.

CHAPTER 7

Checking the form. The application form could certainly be improved.

- **Post applied for**
  Include full title of the post not just the reference number.

- **Place of birth**
  There are several places called Whitchurch. Which county is this one in?

- **Education**
  Primary school qualifications could well be omitted altogether. Examination grades and class of degree should be included.

- **Employment history**
  It would be worthwhile including a few part-time and vacation jobs to show he is no stranger to the world of work.

- **Hobbies, etc**
  Rather superficial and uninteresting. It would be worth mentioning membership of any clubs and any positions held (*eg* Captain of the Clapham South Residents Badminton Team).

- **Illnesses**
  These are not serious enough to rate a mention.

- **Convictions**
  Parking fines are for minor offences and need not be included.

- **Referees**
  What are their titles? What are their telephone numbers? Although not asked for it might be sensible to mention their professions.

- **Why you want the job**
  Not a very convincing or positive reason. There is no need to mention the previous post. This is a chance for Mr Robinson to sell himself and indicate his enthusiasm for the job, but he fails miserably. What exactly are the skills he wants to make better use of?

CHAPTER 8

Interview Questions

Why do you want this job?
Stress the opportunities it offers, not the salary.

Where do you see yourself in five years' time?
Running the whole show, of course. The question is designed to discover whether you are ambitious.

Why should we offer you the job?
Because you have drive, initiative, good qualifications and experience.

What are your strengths/weaknesses?
Concentrate on your strengths. Gloss over the weaknesses.

What do you consider your greatest achievement so far?
This needs to be work-related. Winning a tiddly-winks championship trophy is not enough.

Why did you leave X? or Why do you want to leave X?
Not because you had a row with your boss, but because there were limited opportunities for promotion and you wished to broaden your experience.

What changes would you institute if you were offered the job?
Be careful. You don't know enough about the company yet to offer an informed opinion.

What do you know about us?
If you have done your research properly, quite a lot. Concentrate on the positive.

What is your opinion of the unions, British management, etc?
Avoid a long tirade for or against. Mention both positive and negative aspects, but point out that things have improved enormously over the past two decades.

What salary are you hoping for?
Was a salary stated in the advertisement? If so, quote it. If not try to read the mind of the interviewer. What figure does he have in mind?

What sort of qualities are needed in this job?
Mention your main strengths.

Which aspects of the job do you feel least competent to tackle?
You cannot think of any.

What additional training will you need to do the job?
A good induction should suffice.

Why did you choose this particular career?
Not because of the money but because it offers challenges and scope for your abilities.

What attracts you to this firm?
A little flattery would not be amiss here.

What type of management style do you favour?
Do not become too theoretical unless you are after an academic post. Most firms prefer practical types.

Which other firms have you applied to?
You do not need to name names. In fact, if you are a trifle unscrupulous, you might give the impression that you have a number of firms interested in you even if this is not quite true. This shows you are a go-getter.

What are your main leisure time pursuits?
These need to be active pursuits, not passive ones like watching TV. There should not be too many of them.

CHAPTER 9

What is negotiable?

Location(s) of work
Normally newly appointed employees are not in a position to choose where they work. For some jobs, however, it may be possible for you to work at least part of the time from home.

Date of commencement of employment
Usually negotiable.

Remuneration
This is sometimes negotiable especially for senior jobs. For many public sector jobs you are paid according to your grade on the salary scale.

Holiday entitlement and pay
Not usually negotiable except perhaps for senior jobs. If you have

already made holiday plans most firms will be prepared to allow you time off.

Period of notice required on either side
Usually this is not negotiable.

Pension scheme
Some people may already be in pension schemes and see little point in joining another one. You do not have to join the pension scheme of your new company, and you should see if you can receive a company contribution to your pension fund in lieu. This seems quite a reasonable request but in bureaucratic organisations it can create technical problems.

Redundancy terms
Some senior managers manage to secure very generous severance payments in their contracts, and this is certainly an ideal to strive for. Normally however you will need to settle for less; indeed for junior posts this would only be the statutory minimum.

Trade union membership
If the organisation is non-union or does not recognise your union there is little you can do.

Private health insurance
If the company is not in the habit of providing private insurance for a person of your rank, there is little you can do.

A company car
Same answer as for the previous item.

Relocation allowance
Some organisations offer good relocation allowances for key staff, and you should find out if you are eligible.

Training allowances
It does no harm to bring this up, since it demonstrates that you are keen to improve yourself. Whether you are eligible or not will depend on the organisation's policy.

A children's creche
If the organisation does not have one already, it is difficult to make the provision of one a condition of employment.

CHAPTER 10

Corporate culture and the individual
1. Someone who is looking for security: *bureaucracy.*
2. Someone who is keen to be involved in making decisions: *democracy* or perhaps a *technocracy.*
3. Someone who likes precise instructions: *bureaucracy.*
4. Some who likes to work independently: *democracy.*
5. Someone who likes to see his efforts bring results: *technocracy* or possibly a *democracy.*
6. Someone who hates taking on responsibility: *autocracy.*
7. Someone who hates change: *bureaucracy.*
8. Someone who adapts easily to new situations: *technocracy.*

You will sometimes find a variety of cultures within one organisation depending on the nature of the work. An R & D department may be a technocracy while the production department is run along more autocratic lines. Also a young dynamic technocratic company may become more bureaucratic as it matures.

CHAPTER 11

How to win promotion
Be helpful to your superiors, peers and subordinates.
Find ways to stand out from your peers and get known to your superiors.
Get a reputation for getting things done.
Demonstrate complete reliability.
Learn to make a good presentation using all the relevant techniques.
Carefully nurture your business friends and contacts.
Never deprecate your colleagues.

These are some of the suggestions listed in *Management Self Assessment System*, A Brearley and D Sewell.

CHAPTER 12

Vocational or not?

Archaeology
Probably not. There are not many openings for archaeologists, but an understanding of the subject would be useful for museum curators.

Business Studies
Yes. Courses of this nature give you a good basic knowledge of the world of commerce and may offer a chance to specialise in marketing, finance, *etc*.

Computer Studies
Yes. Information Technology is transforming our lives and a person with a good basic knowledge can go far.

Dentistry
Yes. All the people who have studied dentistry go on to become dentists.

English
Not really. However, a good English qualification would be a good basis if you are contemplating a career in publishing, theatre, teaching, journalism, or any area where communication is important.

French
Not on its own, except for jobs as a translator or interpreter. However a knowledge of foreign languages is important in international commerce and enables you to work in French speaking countries.

Garden Design
It could be, if your course has a strong practical component.

History
Probably not, unless you are very good at it. However, a good understanding of history could be useful in diplomacy, museum work and work involving analytical ability.

International Relations
It could be, especially if you are interested in working for an international organisation or as a diplomat.

Journalism
Yes. Most courses have a strong practical bent and prepare you for a job working in the media or public relations.

Law
Yes. A good basis for all manner of professions (*eg* the law itself, company administration, public administration).

Mathematics
Yes, on the whole. A good grounding in mathematics is the ideal entree to a number of professions requiring high levels of numeracy.

CHAPTER 13

Who experiences stress?

1. Miner	6. Nurse	11. Accountant or estate
2. Policeman	7. Fireman	agent
3. Dentist	8. Professional sportsman	12. Optician
4. Actor	9. Bus driver	13. Vicar
5. Doctor	10. Publisher	14. Librarian

There are a few surprises here. However in all professions there is considerable variation and you may find a London bus driver experiences more stress than a country doctor.

CHAPTER 14

Pruning your expenditure

Household expenditure
This might increase, since you will be spending more time at home. You may able to cut down on your grocery bill by shopping at markets, buying 'own brand' products, restricting your purchases to items on your shopping list and resisting the temptation to buy on impulse.

Mortgage repayments
There may be a way of reducing or rescheduling mortgage repayments, but you need to contact your building society or bank manager and explain the situation. You could, for example:

— make interest-only repayments
— extend the term of your mortgage
— have your repayments suspended for a time
— claim on a redundancy insurance policy, if you have one.

You may be eligible to have the interest on your mortgage paid by the Benefits Agency if your capital falls below a certain level.

Rent
If your savings are below a certain level you may be entitled to have some or all of your rent paid by the Benefits Agency.

Community charge
Again, you may be entitled to a rebate or reduction by applying to your local district council.

Personal transport
You may need your car for travelling to job interviews so only get rid of it if you are desperate. An alternative might be to trade down for an economy model, or to become a one car family.

Insurance and pensions payments
Keep up with them if you can; otherwise explain your predicament to the company or agent concerned and ask him to come up with an acceptable solution.

Subscriptions, fees
These need to be reviewed. Subscriptions to professional organisations and other bodies which might be of use to you should be retained where possible.

Personal expenses (clothes, toiletries, etc)
Do not skimp on your appearance. Suits bought from the Age Concern shop are not an option.

Entertainment and social activities
Do not cut out your social life altogether, though dinners in expensive restaurants and luxury cruises in the Caribbean will need to be put aside for a while. Theatres and recreation centres often offer discounts to the unwaged, and you might wish to take advantage of these.

Loan or credit repayments
If you reckon you will have problems in continuing these, talk to the company or bank concerned. If you can pay off the debt with your redundancy settlement you should do so. Otherwise there may be ways of reducing the payments for a period.

Rental charges
If you are renting equipment decide whether it is absolutely essential. If so and you have problems in paying the charges, discuss the matter with the rental company concerned.

One item will be reduced without any initiative on your part eventually: your income tax liability!

CHAPTER 15

actuary:	numerate, analytical
bursar:	numerate, systematic
debt counsellor:	numerate, communicative, analytical
designer:	creative, practical
health service manager:	analytical, executive, communicative
laboratory technician:	scientific, practical
social worker:	philanthropic
surveyor:	open air, analytical
theatre manager:	executive, communicative
tour guide:	gregarious, communicative

These are suggestions, not definitive answers.

CHAPTER 16

Assessing your suitability

Adaptability
Absolutely vital if you are planning to go to a country which is quite unlike your own.

Health
Some countries are health hazards. If your own health is less than robust you should avoid these.

Language skills
If you are off to a country where the mother tongue is not English you will probably need to know the language.

Resourcefulness
This is a useful attribute especially if you are heading for the Third World.

Stability
Adapting to a different way of life can be stressful, so you need to be a very stable person.

Qualifications
Most countries will not issue you with a visa unless they are satisfied with your qualifications.

Experience abroad
This can be useful, even if it is not work experience. If you have
survived in one foreign country the chances are you will survive in
another.

Patience
This can be a virtue, especially when dealing with bureaucracy
abroad.

Tact
Bluntness has to be avoided. People are often very touchy especially
when they are told off by foreigners.

Tolerance
If you have no respect for the people with whom you will be working
you may feel ill at ease with them.

How did you score?

Over 40	You should have few difficulties in settling down abroad
30-40	A detailed briefing should help you overcome most problems
20-29	A reasonable score, but you should take advice on those attributes where you scored badly
10-19	You will find difficulty in coming to terms with your new situation
Under 10	Stay at home, or you will cause an international incident.

CHAPTER 17

Skills needed to become an entrepreneur

Marketing skills
This is one area where new businesses tend to fall down. You need to
get yourself known through mailshots, advertisements, but best of all
by personal recommendation.

Financial acumen
Your principal objective must be to make a profit, and you need to
keep a tight rein on the costs.

Capital
You need some capital to start off with, even if this means taking out

a second mortgage on your house. If you finance your venture entirely from loans and overdrafts it is your bank which is reaping the profits, not yourself.

Technical expertise
You need to know what you are about, otherwise your competitors will be able to run rings round you.

Organisational skills
Organisations — even if they are only one man bands — have to be managed properly. The alternative is chaos.

Health
Self-employment often means long hours and you need to have plenty of energy and stamina.

Initiative
If you are in charge, you have to take the initiative, not follow others.

Persistence
Remember the legend of Robert the Bruce and the spider. Do not be put off by failure. If your business plan is sound your hard work and dogged determination will be crowned with success.

Motivation
You must be sure that this is something you really want to do, otherwise you will be half-hearted in your efforts.

Self-confidence
You must have enough confidence in yourself to take risks. If you cannot make decisions your business will falter.

How did you score?

40-50	You have the makings of a successful entrepreneur.
30-39	You could do quite well, but pay attention to the areas where your score was low.
20-29	You could succeed but you ought to take advice and perhaps attend a small business course.
10-19	Not really an option for you unless you find an experienced business partner.
0-9	Self-employment is definitely not an option for you.

CHAPTER 18

Changing our ideas

The 5 day week
Many of the jobs in the growth areas (*eg* tourism, security, retailing) require more flexible work patterns. With increasing information technology the number of 9-5 jobs is likely to decline.

A career for life
Fixed period contracts are increasingly common these days especially for senior posts. This means that your future job progression is not guaranteed and you cannot afford to be complacent.

One job per person
Increasingly people may find it is to their advantage to have a portfolio of jobs. Thus if you are made redundant from one you have another to fall back on.

Promotion ladders
If you wish to progress in your career you may well have to move, rather than stay with the same firm. With flatter, less bureaucratic staff structures the scope for actual promotion within a firm may be limited.

Retirement age
The official retirement age (*ie* the age when you become eligible for the state pension) is likely to go up as people live longer. Already in the USA and Singapore it is 67. In actual practice the age at which people finish work will be more fluid.

Casual and part-time jobs
There is considerable growth in these kinds of jobs as the service industries expand. While many are low paid, low status jobs, some will be specialist staff who offer backup to companies as and when needed. These could form part of a job portfolio (see above and Chapter 17).

Retraining
This will be essential for people of all ages as many jobs will either become obsolete or change beyond recognition.

Working in offices and factories
Thanks to information technology and better communications, there will be less need to go in to work these days. Offices may be used as meeting places but little else; most of the work can be done from home workstations with videophones and electronic mailing systems. Factories are a different matter, but with increasing automation the number of factory employees is set to fall.

Company loyalty
You will go where the work is and feel no compunction about staying with the same firm for reasons of loyalty. In a rapidly changing business world with acquisitions, mergers, takeovers and business failures, the firm may not be able to reciprocate this loyalty over the longer term.

Self-employment
There has been a big increase in self-employment in recent years, and this looks set to continue. Eventually people may have a choice of either being employed or contracting out their services to their employers at a higher fee, in the interest of great work flexibility. The advantage of self-employment, of course, is that you are very much in charge of your destiny.

Useful Addresses

The dialling codes are the new ones that will be effective from September 1994 (and mandatory after April 1995).

CAREERS COUNSELLING

(Note E = executive level only; O also outplacement)

Career Analysts, 90 Gloucester Place, London W1H 4BL. Tel: (0171) 935 5452.

Career Counselling Services, 46 Ferry Road, London SW13 9PW. Tel: (0181) 741 0335.

Career Select, 2 Strangeways Villas, Truro, Cornwall TR1 2PA. Tel: (01872) 41355.

Chusid Lander, 25-37 Fitzroy Street, London W1P 5AF. Tel: (0171) 580 6771. Branches in Belfast, Birmingham, Bristol, Glasgow, Manchester, Nottingham. E.

Connaught Executive Career Services Ltd, 32 Savile Row, London W1X 1AG. Tel: (0171) 734 3879. Branches in Birmingham, Bristol, Dublin, Guildford, Leeds, Maidenhead, Manchester, Newcastle, Nottingham and Southampton. EO.

Escape Committee, Tregeraint House, Zennor, St Ives, Cornwall. Tel: (01736) 797061.

Fletcher Hunt & Associates, 59 Devonshire Street, London W1N 1LT. Tel: (0171) 436 8886. Branches in Birmingham, Bournemouth, Dublin, Edinburgh, Glasgow, London, Newcastle, Norwich, Swindon, Wigan and Middle East. EO.

GHN, 16 Hanover Square, London W1R 9AJ. Tel: (0171) 493 5239. E.

Independent Assessment & Research Centre, 17 Portland Place, London W1N 3AF. Tel: (0171) 935 2373.

Jo Ouston & Co, 51-52 Keys House, Dolphin Square, London SW1V 3LX. Tel: (0171) 821 8299.

Mid-Career Development Centre, 1st Floor, 429 Brighton Rd, Croydon CR2 6UD. Tel: (0181) 763 1973.

New Careers, Beaufort Court, Admirals Way, London E14 9XL. Tel: (0171) 515 1222.

New Horizons Career Consultancy Lrd, 41 Dyke Road, Brighton BN1 3JA. Tel: (01273) 748880.

SAS Methven Ltd, 12 Wigmore St. London W1H 9DE. Tel: (0171) 636 1791. Branches in Aldershot, Altrincham, Bristol, Glasgow, Hemel Hempstead, Leeds. E.

Vocational Guidance Association, 7 Harley House, Upper Harley Street, London NW1 4RP. Tel: (0171) 935 2600.

British Association for Counselling, 1 Regent Place, Rugby CV21 2PJ. Tel: (01788) 578328. The Counselling at Work Division of this organisation maintains a register of members who offer career counselling services.

Scottish Association for Counselling, Queen Margaret College, Clerwood Terrace, Edinburgh EH12 8TS. Tel: (0131) 339 8111.

Northern Ireland Association for Counselling, Bryson House, 28 Bedford Street, Belfast BT2 7PE. Tel: (01232) 325835.

The Officers' Association, 48 Pall Mall, London SW1Y 5JY. Tel: (0171) 930 0125. A resettlement agency for people who have served as officers in HM Forces.

EDUCATION

Birkbeck College, Malet Street, London WC1E 7HX. Tel: (0171) 637 9563.

Business and Technician Education Council (BTEC) Central House, Upper Woburn Place, London WC1H 0HH. Tel: (0171) 388 3288.

City and Guilds of London Institute, 76 Portland Place, London W1N 4AA. Tel: (0171) 580 3050.

Council for the Accreditation of Correspondence Colleges, 27 Marylebone Road, London NW1 5JS. Tel: (0171) 935 5391.

ECCTIS, Fulton House, Jessop Avenue, Cheltenham GL50 3SH. Tel: (01242) 518724. Computerised course information service.

Higher Education Advice and Planning Service, 200 Greyhound Road, London W14 9RY. Tel: (0181) 385 3377. Fax: (0181) 381 3377.

National Council for Vocational Qualifications, 222 Euston Road, London NW1 2BZ. Tel: (0171) 387 9898.

The Open College, St Pauls, 781 Wilmslow Rd, Didsbury, Manchester M20 2RW. Tel: (0161) 434 0007.

The Open University, PO Box 71, Walton Hall, Milton Keynes MK7 6AG. Tel: (01908) 74066.

Royal Society of Arts, 8 John Adams Street, London WC2N 6EZ. Tel: (0171) 930 5115.

University and Colleges Admission Service (UCAS), PO Box 28, Cheltenham, Glos GL50 1HY. Tel: (01242) 222444.

National Business Language Information Service, CILT, 20 Bedfordbury, London WC2N 4LB. Tel: (0171) 359 5131.

National Institute of Adult Education, 19B De Montfort Street, Leicester LE1 7GE. Tel: (01533) 551451.

Secretary for External Students, University of London, Senate House, Malet Street, London WC1E 7HU. Tel: (0171) 636 8000.

Workers Educational Association, 9 Upper Berkeley Street, London W1H
   8BY. Tel: (0171) 402 5608.

Residential colleges for adult education
Coleg Harlech, Harlech, Gwynedd LL46 2PU. Tel: (01766) 780363.
Cooperative College, Stanford Hall, Loughborough LE12 5QR. Tel: (01509)
   822333.
Fircroft College, 1018 Bristol Road, Selly Oak, Birmingham B29 6LH. Tel:
   (0121) 472 0116.
Hillcroft College, South Bank, Surbiton, Surrey KT6 6DF. Tel: (0181) 399
   2688.
Newbattle Abbey, Dalkeith, Midlothian EH22 3LL. Tel: (0131) 662 1921.
Northern College, Wentworth Castle, Stainborough, Barnsley, S Yorks S75
   3ET. Tel: (01226) 285426.
Plater College, Pullens Road, Oxford OX3 0DT. Tel: (01865) 741626.
Ruskin College, Walton Street, Oxford OX1 2HE. Tel: (01865) 54331.

SELF-EMPLOYMENT

Association of British Chambers of Commerce, 9 Tufton St, London SW1P
   3QB. Tel: (0171) 222 1555.
British Franchise Association, Thames View, Newtown Road, Henley on
   Thames RG9 1HG. Tel: (01491) 578049.
Business in the Community, 8 Stratton St, London W1X 5FD. Tel: (0171) 629
   1000. This is the umbrella organisation for local enterprise agencies.
Confederation of British Industry (Small Firms Unit), Centre Point, 103 New
   Oxford Street, London WC1 1DU. Tel: (0171) 379 7400.
Co-operative Development Agency, Broadmead House, 21 Panton Street,
   London SW1 4DR. Tel: (0171) 839 2988.
Council for Small Industries in Rural Areas, 141 Castle Street, Salisbury SP1
   3PT. Tel: (01722) 336255.
Head Start in Business, Peter Runge House, 3 Carlton House Terrace, London
   SW1 5DG. Tel: (0171) 839 4300. Help for the under 40s.
The Prince's Youth Business Trust, 5 Cleveland Place, London SW1Y 6JJ.
   Tel: (0171) 925 2900. Help for people under 26.
National Federation of Self-Employed & Small Businesses Ltd, 32 St Anne's
   Road West, Lytham St Anne's, Lancs. Tel: (01253) 720911.

WOMEN

Career Development Centre for Women, 97 Mallard Place, Twickenham,
   Middlesex TW1 4SW. Tel: (0171) 892 3806.
Equal Opportunities Commission, Overseas House, Quay Street, Manchester
   M3 3HN. Tel: (0161) 833 9244.
National Advisory Centre on Careers for Women, 2 Valentine Place, London
   SE1 8QH. Tel: (0171) 401 2280.

Women in Management Association, 64 Marryat Road, London SW19 5BW. Tel: (0181) 944 6332.

WORKING ABROAD

Centre for International Briefing, Farnham Castle, Farnham, Surrey GU9 0Ag. Tel: (01252) 721194.

Christians Abroad, 1 Stockwell Green, London SE9 9HP. Tel: (0171) 737 7811. Also 121 George Street, Edinburgh EH2 4YN.

Employment Conditions Abroad, Anchor House, 15 Britten Street, London SW3 3TY. Tel: (0171) 351 7151.

Expat Network, International House, 500 Purley Way, Croydon, Surrey CR0 4NZ. Tel: (0181) 760 5100. Fax: (0181) 760 0469.

Overseas Development Administration, Abercrombie House, Eaglesham Road, East Kilbride G75 8EA. Tel: (013552) 41199.

Women's Corona Society (Corona Worldwide), Room 3/5, 35 Belgrave Square, London SW1X 8QB. Tel: (0171) 235 1230. Briefings and country reports.

MISCELLANEOUS

British Executive Service Overseas, 164 Vauxhall Bridge Road, London SW1V 2RB. Tel: (0171) 630 0644.

Commission for Racial Equality, Elliot House, 10-12 Allington Street, London SW1E 5EH. Tel: (0171) 828 7022.

Grey Matters, Prestage Street, Old Trafford, Manchester M16 9LH. Tel: (0161) 226 6966. Employment agency.

National Council for Voluntary Organisations, Regents Wharf, 8 All Saints Road, London N1 9RL. Tel: (0171) 713 6161.

Retired Executives Action Clearing House (REACH), 89 Southwark Street, London SE1 0HD. Tel: (0171) 928 0452.

Bibliography

Dialling codes are the ones effective from September 1994 (and mandatory after April 1995).

CAREERS BOOK SERIES

The following publishers publish a wide range of books on different careers, many of them aimed at school or college leavers. However, much of the information provided on individual careers would also be of interest to the older job seeker who may be considering a change of direction.

Association of Graduate Careers Advisory Services (AGCAS), Armstrong House, Oxford Road, Manchester M1 7ED. Tel: (0161) 236 9816. Publishes an extensive range of careers information booklets aimed at students finishing higher education but also of relevance to sixth formers and mature job seekers.

Careers and Occupational Information Centre (COIC), Moorfoot, Sheffield S1 4PQ. Tel: (01742) 704563. Many of the titles are aimed at pupils in schools including the *Working in. . .* and *Skills for. . . series*. The *What else. . .* series however caters for people in certain professions (nurses, teachers, secretaries *etc*) who may be contemplating a career change. Also distributes *Career Builder*, a computer software package.

Careers in Focus, 94 Hagley Road, Birmingham B168LU. Tel: (0121) 455 6611. Publishes a series of videos on careers for school leavers, which are marketed by COIC (see above).

Careers Research and Advisory Service (CRAC). See Hobsons.

Cassell Ltd, Villiers House, Strand, London WC2 5JE. Tel: (0171) 839 4000. Publishes a series of job guides entitled *Getting Jobs in . . .* in addition to the well established *Careers Encyclopedia*.

Hobsons Ltd, Bateman Street, Cambridge CB2 1LZ. Tel: (01223) 354551. Publishes a number of careers books and directories in association with CRAC.

How To Books Ltd, Plymbridge House, Estover Road, Plymouth PL6 7PZ.
Tel: (01752) 695745. Publishes several books offering careers advice especially on careers abroad. (See page facing title page of this book for current
list of titles).

Kogan Page Ltd, 120 Pentonville Road, London N1 9JN. Tel: (0171) 278
0433. Caters for all age groups in its wide range of titles, including the *Jobs
in. . ., Careers in. . .,* and *Working for Yourself* series.

Northcote House Ltd, Plymbridge House, Estover Road, Plymouth PL6 7PZ.
Tel: (01752) 695745. Publishes a number of careers titles.

Newpoint Publishing Co Ltd, Windsor Court, East Grinstead House, East Grinstead RH16 1XA. Tel: (01342) 318265. Publishes some careers directories.

Trotman & Co Ltd, 12-14 Hill Rise, Richmond, Surrey TW10 6UA. Tel:
(0181) 940 5668. Many of the titles seem to be aimed at sixth formers. The
company publishes a catalogue of careers books by a range of publishers
and operates a mail order service.

Vacation Work Publications, 9 Park End Street, Oxford OX1 1HJ. Tel: (01865)
241978. Publishes a number of directories aimed principally at students and
young people wishing to work overseas.

Directories
Many of these are available for consultation at reference libraries and careers
advisory centres as well as being obtainable from bookshops.

British Companies Index (Moodies Services, annual).
British Middle Market Directory Dun & Bradstreet, annual).
Careers Encyclopedia, Segal A & Lea K (Cassell, 1993).
CEPEC Recruitment Guide (Centre for Professional Employment Counselling,
Kent House, 41 East Street, Bromley, Kent BR1 1QQ).
DOG – Directory of Opportunities for Graduates (Newpoint, annual) 7 vols.
Directory of Jobs & Careers Abroad: De Fries A (Vacation Work, 1993).
Directory of Work & Study in Developing Countries, Leppard D (Vacation
Work, 1986).
Handbook of Free Careers Information in the UK (Trotman, 1987).
International Directory of Voluntary Work: Woodworth D (ed) (Vacation
Work, 1989).
International Recruitment Guide & Directory, Cunningham M (International
Venture Handbooks/How To Books, 1995).
Occupations (COIC, annual)
Offbeat Careers, Donald V. (Kogan Page, 1990).
Register of Graduate Employment & Training (AGCAS, Association of Grad-
uate Careers Advisory Services, annual).

Volunteer Work Abroad, Sewell H (Central Bureau for Educational Visits & Exchanges, 1986).
The Executive Grapevine, Baird R S & Hickson J M
The Times 100 Leading Companies (Times Newspapers Ltd, annual).
Yearbook of Recruitment & Employment Services, Federation of Recruitment & Employment Services (Longman, annual).

Periodicals
Careerscope, Independent Schools Careers Organisation (Hobsons). Careers magazine for school leavers.
Escape: The Career Changers Magazine, Weavers Press, Tregeraint House, Zennor, St Ives, Cornwall TR26 3DB. Tel: (01736) 797061. Magazine for career changers.
Graduate Careers (Dominion Press). Magazine for recent graduates.
Graduate Post (Newpoint). A jobs paper for recent graduates.
Job Finder, Overseas Consultants, PO Box 152, Douglas, Isle of Man. Fortnightly overseas jobs newsletter.
Overseas Jobs Express, Island Publishing, PO Box 22, Brighton BN1 6HX. Tel: (01273) 440229. Fortnightly overseas jobs paper.
Nexus, Expat Network, 500 Purley Way, Croydon CR0 4NZ. Tel: (0181) 760 5100. Monthly overseas jobs magazine.
Returners (Hobsons). A magazine for women returning to work.
School Leaver (Dominion Press). Careers magazine for school leavers.
Springboard (Hobsons/CRAC). Careers magazine for school leavers.
Technology Graduate (Newpoint). Magazine for technology graduates.

Jobhunting & careers advice
Employment for the Disabled, Thompson M (Kogan Page, 1986).
Great Answers to Tough Interview Questions, Yate M J (Kogan Page, 1992).
How to Choose a Career, Donald V (Kogan Page, 1993).
How to Face the Interview, Fletcher C (Unwin Paperbacks, 1986).
How to Pass that Interview, Johnstone J (How To Books, 2nd edition 1994).
How to Win at the Job Game, Parsons E J (Kogan Page, 1983).
Job Search — The Video, Valart Ltd, PO Box 4, Rowlands Castle, Hants PO9 6BR. Tel: (01705) 413162.
Test your own Aptitude, Barrett J and Williams G (Kogan Page, 1990).
The Good Guide to the Job Interview, Sound & Vision, 2 Hill Grove, Caswell, Swansea SA3 4RQ (video).
The Perfect CV, Eggert M (Century Business, 1992).
The Perfect CV, Jackson T (Piatkus, 1991).
The Right Way to Write Your Own CV, Clarke J (Elliot Right Way Books, 1989).
Unqualified Success, Gabriel J (Penguin, 1986).
What Colour is Your Parachute, Bolls R N & Snow T (Ten Speed Press, 1992).
Your First Job, Page A (Kogan Page, 1984).

Career change
Career Change, Morphy L (CRAC/Hobsons, 1987).
Changing Your Job after 35, Golzen G (Kogan Page, 1988).
Getting a Better Job, Courtis J (IPM, 1993).
How to Get a Job after 45, Bayley J (Kogan Page, 1990).
How to Start a New Career, Johnstone J (How To Books, 2nd edition 1994).
Job Hunting after 50, Ray S N (Wiley, 1991).
The Mid-Career Action Guide, Kemp D & F (Kogan Page, 1992).

Education
Business and Management Courses — The Way In, Heap B (Trotman, 1992).
How to Choose your Degree Course, Heap B (Trotman, 1991).
How to Master Languages, Jones R (How To Books, 1993).
Mature Students' Handbook, Rosier I and Earnshaw L (Trotman, 1989).
Part-time Degrees, Diplomas and Certificates (CRAC Hobson).
Second Chances, Pates A & Good M (COIC, 1990).
The Kogan Page Mature Student's Handbook, Korving M (Kogan Page, 1991).
University Entrance — The Official Guide (Association of Commonwealth Universities, 1993).
Which Degree? (Trotman, 1993)
Which Subject? Which Career? Jamieson A (Consumers Association/CRAC, 1992).

Self-employment
A Guide to Franchising, Mendelsohn M (Pergamon, 1984).
Croner's Reference Book for the Self-Employed and Small Businesses (Croner Publications).
Going Freelance, Golzen G (Kogan Page, 1989).
How to Buy and Run a Shop, Maitland I (How To Books, 2nd edition, 1992).
How to Buy and Run a Small Hotel, Parker K (How To Books, 1992).
How to Start a Business from Home, Jones G (How To Books, 3rd edition 1994).
How to Work from Home, Phillipson I (How To Books, 1992).
Independent Careers, Boehm K and Lees-Spalding J (Bloomsbury, 1992).
Occupation — Self Employed, Pettit R (Wildwood House, 1981).
Starting a Business, Hargreaves R (Heinemann, 1987).
Starting Your Own Business (Consumers Association, 1988).
The Entrepreneur's Complete Assessment Guide, Gray D (Kogan Page, 1987).
The Little Business Book, Hingston P (Hingston, 5 The Roundel, Auchterarder, Perthshire PH3 1PU, 1988).
Working for Yourself, Golzen G (Kogan Page, 1992).

Working abroad
How to Emigrate, Jones R (How To Books, 1994).
How to Get a Job Abroad — A Handbook of Opportunities and Contacts, Jones R (How To Books, 3rd edition 1994). Contains extensive bibliography.

How to Get a Job in America, Jones R (How To Books, 2nd edition 1994).
How to Get a Job in Australia, Vandome N (How To Books, 1992).
How to Get a Job in Europe, Hempshell M (How To Books, 2nd edition 1994).
How to Spend a Year Abroad, Vandome N (How To Books, 2nd edition 1994).
How to Teach Abroad — A Guide to Opportunities Worldwide, Jones R (How To Books, 2nd edition 1994).
Mind your Manners — Managing Culture Clash in the Single European Market, Mole J (Nicholas Brealey Publishing, 1992).
Opportunities Overseas, Harper A (Grant Dawson, 1992).
Working Abroad, Golzen G (Kogan Page, 1992).
Working Abroad: Essential Financial Advice for Expatriates and their Employers (International Venture Handbooks/How To Books, 1993).

Women
Equal Opportunities — A Careers Guide, Alston A & Miller R (Penguin, 1992).
Getting There — Job Hunting for Women, Wallis M (Kogan Page, 1990).
New Mothers at Work, Bannen J & Moss P (Unwin, 1988).
Returners, National Advisory Centre on Careers for Women (1990).
Returning to Work, Women Returners' Network (Longman, 1990).
The Juggling Act, Katz A (Bloomsbury, 1992).
Women at Work, Clarke D (Element Books, 1990).
Women Can Return to Work, Steel M & Thornton Z (Grapevine).
Women Working Out, Chapman J (COIC, 1991).

Financial matters
Supplementary Benefits Handbook (Dept of Social Security/HMSO).
The Hutchinson Money Manager, Allen M (Hutchinson, 1987).
The Guardian Money Guide, Dibben M (Collins, 1988).

Miscellaneous
Executive Leadership, Jaques E & Clement S D (Blackwell, 1991).
How to Succeed at Work, Orr F (Unwin Paperbacks, 1987).
Life, Work and Livelihood in the Third Age: Final Report (Carnegie UK Trust, 1993).
Management Self-Assessment System, Brearley A & Sewell D (Ernst & Young, 1990).
Smart Moves, Golzen G & Garner A (Kogan Page, 1991).
The 100 Best Companies to Work For in the UK, Reynolds B (Fontana, 1989).
The Age of Unreason, Handy C (Business Books, 1989).
The Peter Principle, Peter L J & Hull R (William Morrow, NY, 1969).
The Social Psychology of Work, Argyle M (Penguin, 1989).
Understanding Organisations, Handy C (1985).
Why Things go Wrong — The Peter Principle Revisited, Peter L J (Allen & Unwin, 1985).

Glossary

appraisal: review of an employee's performance usually conducted by a superior.

aptitude: natural ability.

brainstorm: group method of solving problems by generating ideas however absurd.

burn out: state of exhaustion sometimes experienced by high fliers.

communication: the exchange of ideas and information.

corporate culture: characteristics which distinguish the behaviour of one organisation from another.

counselling: advice on how to cope with problems.

deskilling: reduction in skills needed for job as a result of increased automation.

downsizing: euphemism for a reduction in staff numbers.

entrepreneur: person who sets up and runs his or her own business.

executive search: the process by which senior managers are approached and recruited.

franchise: A concession to run a business

high flier: talented person who is marked out for high office in the future.

golden handshake: redundancy payment.

golden hello: payment made to attract a person to a particular job.

job satisfaction: being happy with your job.

job security: having a job which is likely to last.

job sharing: system under which two people share the same job.

knowledge workers: people who process information such as teachers, writers, publishers, lawyers, systems analysts, accountants, managers etc.

mentor: an experienced older manager who assists younger staff with their career progress.

mid-life crisis: a feeling that you are not getting anywhere, usually experienced in mid-career.

motivation: incentive.

network: a group of people with a special relationship with others from a similar background.

networking: using a network of contacts to discover career opportunities.

OTE: on target earnings (ie including commission/bonus payments)

outplacement: process whereby consultants find jobs often for redundant employees.

plateau: no further prospects of promotion.

psychometric tests: pencil and paper tests designed to discover a person's skills and aptitudes.

stress: illness brought about by excessive pressure.

transferable skills: skills that are useful in a wide range of jobs.

values: a broad tendency to prefer certain states of affairs over others.

visibility: being noticed by your superiors.

vocational qualifications: qualifications oriented towards particular careers.

Index